D1082315

SECRET WISDOM

SECRET WISDOM

OCCULT SOCIETIES AND ARCANE KNOWLEDGE THROUGH THE AGES

RUTH
CLYDESDALE

To the Memory of my Parents

PICTURE CREDITS

All pictures courtesy of Shutterstock and Creative Commons.

This edition published in 2021 by Arcturus Publishing Limited
26/27 Bickels Yard, 151–153 Bermondsey Street,
London SE1 3HA

Copyright © Arcturus Holdings Limited

All rights reserved. No part of this publication may be reproduced,
stored in a retrieval system, or transmitted, in any form or by any means,
electronic, mechanical, photocopying, recording or otherwise, without
prior written permission in accordance with the provisions of the
Copyright Act 1956 (as amended). Any person or persons who do any
unauthorised act in relation to this publication may be liable to criminal
prosecution and civil claims for damages.

AD007742UK

Printed in the UK

CONTENTS

Hermes, the god who guides souls on their way back to the Divine. His message tells us to worship in silence ('Silentium deum cole').

INTRODUCTION

I give you the end of a golden string,
Only wind it into a ball,
It will lead you in at Heaven's gate
Built in Jerusalem's wall.
— William Blake,
To the Christians

KNOWLEDGE, understanding, wisdom – they are like rivers running through the course of human history. Sometimes they flow above ground, other times they plunge beneath the surface and flow on quietly as if lost. But sooner or later real wisdom surfaces again, in another country and a different age.

The particular current of wisdom that concerns us was enshrined in the Mystery cults of ancient Greece. Today the word 'mystery' has a rather different meaning from that which it held for our Greek ancestors. We think it denotes a puzzle to be solved, something that keeps us guessing until we've cracked it. But to the ancients it was something more profound. 'Mystery' is related to 'mystic'. Being a participant in one of the Mysteries made you a mystic: it was an initiation into knowledge of other worlds and different dimensions. And it changed you for life.

This ancient wisdom reveals the true nature of what it means to be human. It is a knowledge that cannot be told – only experienced. Participants in the Greek Mysteries were sworn to silence, and their wisdom has remained hidden from most of humanity ever since. Yet throughout the ages, enough individuals have re-created the Mystery experience in various ways for us to be able to describe its contents.

Exploring the flow of the secret wisdom can be exhilarating, and it may even lead you closer to experiencing it yourself. This book will take you through two and a half millennia of time and several different cultures. Although it cannot provide a comprehensive list of all the mystics who have preserved the hidden wisdom, it will give you a variety of viewpoints from which to regard the ancient Mysteries – and you might even realize that you yourself can become a link in the Golden Chain of those who have penetrated the secret.

OUR STORY BEGINS with a song. In a way, it is the most famous song of all time, one that is still echoing through our lives now. It is being sung by Orpheus, the archetypal musician and poet. He is sitting in a wild landscape in the north of Greece, and he is accompanying himself on a lyre. The song is so beautiful that it affects even animals, which cluster round to listen. In his most inspired moments, Orpheus can sing so powerfully that the rocks themselves strain to move closer to him. But Orpheus is more than just a musician – he is a shaman, a priest, and the discoverer of a new way of putting meaning into life.

> I am a child of Earth and starry Heaven
> — *Orphic Gold Tablets*

THE LIFE OF ORPHEUS

Orpheus is not a historical figure but a mythical one, whose life and death are said to have taken place in the time of the Heroes in Greece. Even to the Greeks of Socrates' time, about five centuries before Christ, he was an ancient and venerated figure who consorted with the likes of Hercules and Jason of Argonaut fame. The first historical mention of Orpheus to come down to us is from a Greek poet, Ibykos, who flourished during the sixth century BCE. He mentions 'famous Orpheus', so by that time Orpheus must have been a well-known figure.

The events and pattern of Orpheus' life, being mythical, are a teaching story from which we can begin to glean just why Orpheus is still a familiar name today. There are various accounts of his parentage, but the most common makes him the son of Oiagros, the king of Thrace, and Kalliope, the Muse of epic poetry. In other versions of the myth, Oiagros is a river-god or Apollo is Orpheus' father, making him fully divine rather than half-human. Whichever version we choose, his inheritance plainly includes skill in poetry, and Apollo recognized his musical skills with the gift of a golden lyre.

The most celebrated events of Orpheus' life are two in number. First, he is said to have travelled with Jason's crew on the ship Argo in their expedition to steal the Golden Fleece from its temple in Colchis. During this voyage, the ship had to sail past the island of the Sirens – bird-like women who would sing with such irresistible enchantment that sailors would try to get as close as possible in order to hear, until their ships were

Magic, poetry and mystery – Orpheus is the archetypal originator of them all. The sound of his lyre playing its famous song still echoes today.

wrecked on the cruel coastal rocks. Orpheus however sang a rival song that surpassed the Sirens' in beauty, persuading the sailors to listen only to him and to pass safely by the deadly lure towards the rocks.

The powerful enchantment of Orpheus' song suggests a magical charm, a bewitchment beyond the usual effect of music. Orpheus was considered to be well versed in all the magical arts – one of the first magicians, in fact.

JOURNEY TO THE UNDERWORLD

The second story in which Orpheus stars is the most famous of all: his attempt to win back his wife Eurydice from the Underworld. Eurydice was bitten by a poisonous snake and died, either while fleeing from the unwanted advances of one of Apollo's sons or while dancing on her wedding day. The distraught Orpheus sang such heart-breaking dirges and laments that the gods themselves advised him to go down to the Underworld and ask the rulers Hades and Persephone to restore Eurydice to life. Alone among men, therefore, he entered the land of death while still alive and returned from it. Hades and Persephone were so moved by his music that they agreed to his request, stipulating only that he should not look back as Eurydice followed him up to the light of day.

We know – or we think we know – that Orpheus either forgot this injunction or could not resist turning round to see if Eurydice truly was following him. Either way, she vanished back into the Underworld, there to stay with the other dead shades. However, there is at least one ancient version of the myth in which he succeeds in his quest, becoming the first person on earth to bring back a human being from the dead.

The more familiar story recounts that from the moment of Eurydice's loss the grief-stricken and guilty Orpheus turned his back on women, devoting himself instead to the beauty of young men. He thus enraged the Thracian Maenads, female followers of the wine-god Dionysus, who attacked him during one of their periods of frenzied worship. When the stones they threw at him refused to hit their target, they set on him with their bare hands and tore him limb from limb. In other versions, the Maenads are infuriated by Orpheus turning from his earlier worship of Dionysus to sun worship. It was his habit to dress in pure white and venerate Apollo, the solar god, every morning from the summit of Mount

Pangaion. Here the Maenads found him and rent him limb from limb.

But this terrible death was not the end of Orpheus – he was, after all, at least half-divine. His head and lyre fell into the river Hebrus and, the head still singing, they were carried into the Mediterranean to be washed ashore on the island of Lesbos. Here they were enshrined, and Orpheus' head gave oracles and prophecies until finally silenced by Apollo. Meanwhile his mother and aunts, the Muses, gathered up the pieces of his body and interred them on the lower slopes of Mount Olympus. Both at the shrine and the tomb, the nightingales were said to sing with special sweetness. And the island of Lesbos became known for its poets, including of course Sappho, who wrote the very first love poetry. Orpheus' lyre was eventually placed in the heavens as the constellation Lyra.

Elements of this tale are to be found in myths of both earlier and later times, indicating that there is something archetypal and universal about it. For example, the ancient Egyptian myth of Osiris tells of Orpheus being dismembered by his enemy Seth, only for his sister/wife Isis to gather together the pieces and revivify the body sufficiently to bear his child, Horus. There is also a story of the Maenads rending to pieces another human being, Pentheus, the king of Thebes. The half-god who suffers a tortuous death only to affirm his continuing life is of course familiar to us through the figure of Christ. We are looking, then, at an archetypal figure, someone who through his songs can move even inert matter and who has power over death itself.

THE BIRTH OF THE WORLD

Once we realize just what Orpheus sang, we can begin to see why such powers were attributed to him. Not much has come down to us, but various philosophers and historians of the early centuries of our era quoted parts of Orpheus' song in their works. Its theme is the birth of the world, creation itself. The story is strange. The world begins (as in Genesis) with darkness and chaos. Chronos, or Time, forms an egg out of the mysterious fifth element, ether. When the egg hatches, the god who emerges is dazzlingly beautiful: he is Phanes (light), Protogonos (first-born) or Eros – Love himself. Phanes gives birth to all the familiar Olympian gods: Zeus, Aphrodite and so forth. But Zeus asks Night how he can overcome Chronos, and the answer is that he must swallow the universe. Amazingly, that is what Zeus does, thus becoming everything. So Orpheus sings:

> Zeus is the first. Zeus, the thunderer, is the last.
> Zeus is the head. Zeus is the middle, and by Zeus all things
>   were fabricated.
> Zeus is male, Immortal Zeus is female.
> Zeus is the foundation of the earth and of the starry heaven.
> Zeus is the breath of all things. Zeus is the rushing of
>   indefatigable fire.
> Zeus is the root of the sea: He is the Sun and Moon.
> Zeus is the king; He is the author of universal life…
> Would you behold his head and his fair face,
> It is the resplendent heaven, round which his golden locks
> Of glittering stars are beautifully exalted in the air.
>
> (Cory, p.290)

The significance of this song may not be apparent at first, but it is tremendous. Here is Orpheus recounting a tale of creation and of a universal god who pervades all being, rendering the world and all that is in it sacred. Such an idea was profoundly different from the Greek religion, which included many gods and was designed to act primarily as a cohesive social force. Orpheus, however, offers individual revelations of truth, and these are to be discovered in a secret way, through initiation and rites.

These rites relate to another myth that is central to the Orphic religion: that of the death of the wine-god Dionysus. According to this tale, Dionysus is the son of Zeus and the goddess of the Underworld, Persephone. Zeus' jealous wife Hera incites the Titans, ancient earth-beings, to kill the child. They disguise themselves by smearing white clay on their faces. Then, as the child Dionysus sits playing with his toys, they surround him and tear him to pieces. Not satisfied with this horrible cruelty, they boil and roast the limbs. As they settle to their gruesome meal, the smell of roasting flesh alerts Zeus. With his lightning he hurls the Titans back into Tartarus, the abyss beneath the Underworld, and saves Dionysus' heart. Steam rising from the singed Titans forms an ash, which Zeus mixes with clay to make the first humans. Hence every human being has a mixed nature, partly primitive and Titanic but – because the

Almighty Zeus uses thunderbolts for weapons to conquer his enemies in the cosmos he's made his own.

Titans ingested some of the child's flesh – partly divine and Dionysian.

For the first time in Greek religion, the idea of a divine spark in humanity hinted that life – true life – resided in the spirit rather than the body. For those who realize this, sensual pleasures begin to lose their charm. The body is seen as imprisoning the soul; there is an Orphic saying: *soma sema*, 'the body is a tomb'. Followers of the Orphic religion believed that life on earth is a punishment for the Titanic part of the human being, and that the Dionysian divine spark in us all longs to be reunited with the source of divinity: the highest god, Zeus.

ORPHIC RITUALS

The Orphic religion enumerated several ways in which that spark could be freed. First, an initiation was required. This may have taken the form of a ritual meal mimicking the death of Dionysus. The form of the initiation appears to have derived from Cretan rites in which a bull was dismembered and eaten raw, the initiates then processing noisily into the countryside with flutes, cymbals and sacred objects. Orphic religion must have adapted this bloody and violent rite, since initiates became dedicated vegetarians. But it is certain that they went through a strangely paradoxical ritual of being smeared with white clay or gypsum in imitation of the Titans, which was considered to be cleansing and purifying. Indeed, the Greek word *apomattein* means both 'to smear' and 'to purify'. This identified the initiate in a vivid and immediate way with both sides of his being, the holy Dionysian and the earth-bound Titanic.

After the initiation, the new Orphic disciple entered upon a life of austerity and self-discipline that was famous throughout the classical world. Never again would he eat meat, for Orphics held to the doctrine of reincarnation for the immortal soul. Nor would he take the life of animals for the purposes of sacrifice. The killing of men, including oneself, was forbidden, for to do so would be to cut short the divinely ordained period of punishment. Orphics wore white to symbolize their desire for purity. Such a religiously inspired way of life with its emphasis on individual responsibility might seem commonplace to us now. Similar procedures can be seen in various religions, particularly in the context of monastic life. Orphism was the very first Western religion to have developed in this way, and to have imposed strictures on the laity. As we shall see in following chapters, it has been – and even to this day, continues to be – profoundly influential on many philosophical and religious movements. This is where religion and spirituality, as we understand it, begins.

THE AFTERLIFE

The question of life after death was more important for followers of Orpheus than for those of the mainstream Greek religion. The common view of death can be seen in Homer's epic poem *The Iliad*. His warrior heroes go into battle with a courage that is all the more impressive because they believe that all light and pleasure is to be found only during the brief years of life. After death they will continue to exist but only in an attenuated way, as ghostly shadows in a gloomy Underworld, able to squeak and gibber but deprived of the power of human speech. In contrast to that bleak outlook, the Orphic religion promised a brighter future. Since the soul reincarnated, death was not a final state. However, since life in the body was a punishment, further lives were to be avoided if possible. The asceticism of the Orphic life was intended to loosen the bonds of the body, moving the focus of attention away from sensual Titanic pleasures and towards the gifts of the Dionysian soul.

Some ancient writers count three lives lived in purity to be sufficient to escape from the wheel of life and death. Others, such as Plato, are less optimistic and reckon that three periods of a thousand years are necessary. Even so, the first-century historian Plutarch and his wife Timoxena, who were both Orphic initiates, found the religion a consolation during times of trouble. And no wonder! The Orphic understanding of the afterlife marks a profound change from the ancient Greek belief that affects life as well. Whereas the Homeric view of the spiritual world encouraged the living to pursue all sensual pleasures while they were still able to do so, Orpheus had taught humans that their true being was a divine spark and that their focus should be on nourishing it by living well. For the first time in history, a human being could take charge of his or her fate. Rather than being a plaything of the gods, there was the belief that he or she belonged among the divine, immortal company of Elysium. That new understanding of the real nature of humanity has resounded through Western religions ever since, though it tends to be hidden away from the masses and revealed only in the mystical traditions.

Illustration of Charon's boat. Created by Feyen-Perrin, it was first published in L'Illustration Journal Universel, Paris, 1857.

The promise that cheered the followers of Orpheus was that of escape from the endless round of reincarnation into an eternity spent in the company of immortal gods and goddesses in the paradisal Elysian Fields. We have some extraordinary evidence as to the nature of the Orphic future life: a number of delicate gold plaques or tablets found in graves at various burial sites in Greece, southern Italy and elsewhere, which seem to date from the fourth century BCE to the third century CE. Inscriptions on them testify to the journey and experiences the Orphics expected to undergo after the moment of death. The dead person is congratulated and reassured, 'Happy and blessed one, thou shalt be god instead of mortal.' Then elaborate instructions are given on the route to be followed to the Elysian Fields ('Go to the right as far as one should go...') and the correct words to be spoken at certain points. The most critical moment arises when the soul encounters two springs, one to the left of the path and the other to the right. The one on the left is Lethe, forgetfulness. If the soul drinks here, it will lose all awareness of its past and be reborn. But the spring on the right is Mnemosyne, memory. Here the soul must announce, 'I am a child of Earth and starry Heaven,' and ask the guards for a drink. It will then be able to pass on along 'the right hand road by holy meadows and groves of Persephone'.

By this means the soul achieves its goal of eternal happiness, and will sing:

> I have flown out of the sorrowful, weary circle
> I have passed with swift feet to the diadem desired.

The soul is liberated, purified into a new state of innocence and completely fulfilled. The inscriptions include a strange yet vivid image to assure the dead person of their future bliss: 'a kid thou art fallen into milk' (Guthrie, p.173).

PURIFICATION AND LIBERATION

The tale of Orpheus is a strange mixture of the tragic and optimistic. He suffered a similar death to the god whose rites were developed into a sophisticated religious philosophy – yet Orpheus, whose death is an integral part of his story, could raise the dead. His influence has two distinct strands. On the one hand, he is revered as a reformer of religion, modifying existing forms of the worship of Dionysus rather than initiating new doctrines. Even the concept of Elysium, as seen on the Orphic gold tablets, already exists in Homer – although in his poetry it is exclusively reserved for the privileged few.

Such is the exoteric side of Orpheus. But there is an esoteric side too. Although we know a little about the Orphic initiation and way of life, much has been lost because initiates adhered very strictly to their vow of secrecy. All we are left with are cryptic statements such as that of Pausinias, the Greek historian of the first century BCE: 'Whoever has seen an initiation at Eleusis, or read the writings called Orphic, knows what I mean' (Guthrie, p.10). Or, a century later, Diodorus wrote of 'the Orphic poems and the things which are introduced in the mysteries, the details of which it is not lawful to recount to the uninitiated' (Guthrie, p.10). It is hard for us to imagine an idea so powerful that it was preserved in virtually unbroken secrecy for centuries, but such is the case with Orphic initiations.

Yet the thread of knowledge that Orphism embodied has persevered in various forms throughout history. One of the ways it has survived is through another form of esotericism: magic. Orpheus, remember, was a singer who could charm the very rocks. Clearly his music had a magical power, and over time many spells, charms and magical invocations were produced in his name. Song itself is so entwined with magic that the link is linguistic, 'enchantment' meaning literally a spell worked by chanting. The root word from which both derive is the Latin *cantare*, meaning to sing or play. Therefore Orpheus was seen as the first and archetypal magician. Eighty-six Orphic hymns attributed to him (although almost certainly dating from the early centuries CE) still exist. These consist of elaborate invocations to a range of gods, some for specific purposes and others for general protection. Most hymns are accompanied by instructions on the correct spice or herb to be burnt as incense. The hymns gained such a reputation for being powerful magical tools that during the Renaissance the philosopher and astrologer Marsilio Ficino considered them too dangerous for publication. Hence the Orphic knowledge remained a hidden current, available only orally to a select band of educated men who probably considered themselves as initiates of a sort.

So Orpheus represents a hidden understanding of the true nature, potential, and ultimate happiness of humankind. On an exoteric level, the myth of Dionysus' untimely death can represent the process of wine-making. Dionysus is destroyed like the grape, but his father Zeus swallows his heart and later impregnates the mortal Semele. After she is destroyed by Zeus' own lightning, he plucks the unborn child from her womb and sews him into his thigh, later giving birth to the second Dionysus. This reborn god becomes the wild wine-god in whose name transgressive rites are performed. But the Orphic understanding of the tale is about spiritual intoxication. Another name for Dionysus is Liber, which means the bringer of freedom. On a mundane level, this can be the loss of inhibition that wine brings, but the true, Orphic liberation is from the suffering of life itself.

Although we will be tracing the course of Orphic wisdom throughout the Western tradition, we should remember that the 'perennial philosophy' is universal in nature. Various religions and cultures express it in different ways, but similarities are apparent. Myth told that Orpheus himself derived his wisdom from studying with the priests of ancient Egypt, whose religion had a strong focus on the nature of life after death. We can also discern deep connections with the tenets of Buddhism. The Buddha, who lived in about the fifth century BCE, outlined his teaching in Four Noble Truths: that life is suffering, that suffering has a beginning and that it has an end. The fourth truth outlines the Noble Eightfold Path that leads to the end of suffering. Orphism agrees on the nature of life and that it has both a cause (given in mythical terms as the death of Dionysus) and an end. The Path that the ascetic initiate follows seems to be less elaborate than the Buddhist Noble Eightfold Path, although there may be much that we do not know. However, both paths have the same purpose, that of purifying the human being by weaning him away from sensory pleasures and improving his moral conduct, thereby strengthening the spiritual life.

ELEUSIS AND THE GODDESS

The Orphic Mysteries were not the only initiatory rites practised in ancient Greece. Closely related and perhaps even more widely known and celebrated were the Eleusinian Mysteries of Demeter and Persephone. These Mysteries are echoed by a practice used particularly in Tibet. In effect, the Eleusinian rites took participants through an experience of

Demeter gives the gift of grain, symbolic of life itself – but her Mysteries involve initiates experiencing a symbolic death before that life is given.

death. Tibetan practitioners will meditate upon *The Tibetan Book of the Dead* and pursue practices mimicking the processes of death for the same purpose: to prepare themselves for the body's death in order to be able to make the correct choices in the afterlife.

According to His Holiness the Dalai Lama, at the point of death the consciousness becomes very clear, so that it is possible to get far closer to the truth of existence than during life. But without preparation, that clarity can be wasted and the person will end up being reincarnated rather than winning freedom from the wheel of birth and death. What's more, experiencing such clear consciousness during life will reveal insights into the person's true nature that will become a source of liberating bliss while they are still alive. As we shall see throughout later chapters, philosophers and mystics have pursued this goal throughout many centuries, but it is at Eleusis that we find the first proof of this spiritual discipline being practised.

We have seen that the Orphic gold tablets outlined the route to be followed through the other world and the words to be spoken. Indeed, Orphic rites could also have dramatized death, but if so we do not have evidence. Of the Eleusinian rites, however, there survive enough hints to give some idea of the dramatic events that participants underwent.

Although the Orphic and Eleusinian Mysteries have points in common, there are many differences as well. The Eleusinian rites are firmly based in one place: Eleusis, near Athens. Originally they were for Athenian citizens only, but as time passed by Greeks from beyond the city were included and eventually even foreigners. The rites were open to slaves and women in an age when such parity was far from being the norm, yet such became their prestige that Roman emperors clamoured for initiation. Like the Orphic rites, they offered an intense individual religious experience, but unlike Orphism the rites did not impose moral obligations. However, those who had committed murder or other bloody crimes could not be admitted without being purified first. The Mysteries were celebrated annually, during which time exiles were allowed to return from abroad and warfare was brought to a temporary truce. That gives some idea of how important the Mysteries were to the Athenians.

As with the Orphic rites, strict secrecy was enjoined upon participants. Perhaps because initiates were so widespread, more hints have come down to us than for the Orphic rites but, all the same, the degree to which secrecy was maintained is remarkable. The rites were regarded as being so precious that they survived an attempt to suppress them in the fifth century and seem to have survived from around 600 BCE to at least the eighth century CE or later.

THE HYMN TO DEMETER

The Eleusinian Mysteries were based on a myth that is perhaps more familiar than that of Dionysus' death, yet it too is concerned with the nature of death and the afterlife. The myth is that of Persephone's rape by Hades and her mother Demeter's search for her missing daughter. The tale is told in a long poem, the Homeric Hymn to Demeter, dating from about the sixth century BCE. Persephone, the lovely daughter of the grain goddess Demeter, is picking flowers one day with some of her friends when Hades, dark ruler of the Underworld, emerges in his chariot from a chasm in the ground and snatches her away to be his bride. Demeter has no idea what has happened to her daughter and, too distraught with fear and grief to eat, searches hopelessly for nine days. Finally the Sun, who sees everything, tells her what happened and that Zeus approved the rape. Demeter comes to Eleusis, where the local king's daughters give her hospitality and persuade her to break her fast, and their nursemaid cheers her with obscene humour. Demeter commands that a temple be built to her. However, she is so angry with Zeus that she causes a famine by forbidding the crops to grow. Zeus sends Hermes down to Hades to bargain for Persephone's return, to which Hades agrees. But he secretly gives Persephone pomegranate seeds to eat, thereby ensuring that she has taken part in Underworld existence and must return. Although Persephone is allowed to re-enter the upper world and Demeter causes the crops to grow again, an annual cycle begins whereby Persephone must return to her husband each autumn.

The myth reflects not only the mystery of seasonal growth, but also the nature of the human soul that undergoes cycle after cycle of suffering, joy and loss. Reincarnation is hinted at, although not explicitly stated. As with the Orphic Mysteries, the initiate is instructed in how to escape from the cycle and achieve ultimate bliss. Eleusis means 'place of happy arrival' and is related to Elysium. The ancients were in no doubt of the Mysteries' efficacy. Cicero considered them to be the most precious aspect of Greek culture, and stated unequivocally, 'In the Mysteries we perceive the real principle of life, and learn not only to live happily, but to die with a fairer hope.'

The Mysteries developed into elaborate and lengthy rites. They comprised two parts, the Lesser Mysteries being celebrated over three days in the spring month of Anthesterion. Little is known of them, but they seem to have been purificatory rites with the story of Persephone at their heart. It was necessary to have taken part in the Lesser Mysteries in order to qualify for participation in the Greater Mysteries, which took place in Boedromion (approximately our September) and lasted ten days. Here, Demeter and the mystery of the grain took precedence. In all, there were three stages of initiation. The Lesser Mysteries offered purification or *katharsis*, while the Greater Mysteries comprised a first initiation (telete) and a final initiation (epopteia) that could only be taken a year after the telete.

While the Orphic Mysteries may have been limited in their appeal because of the strictures of the Orphic way of life, the Eleusinian Mysteries seem to have had the character of a social gathering, virtually a holiday. The Lesser Mysteries took place near the river Ilissos, and included bathing in the river. There were also sacrifices and dancing, and sacred objects hidden in baskets hinted at hidden meanings yet to be revealed.

GREATER MYSTERIES OF DEMETER

The more elaborate Greater Mysteries of Demeter began with holy objects from Eleusis being brought to Demeter's temple in Athens. On the second day, the cry of 'Halade Mystae' urged the participants (mystae) down to the sea to bathe and purify themselves. The peculiar habit of taking along a small pig appears to have arisen from the belief that pigs absorb evil, an idea that occurs in the Gospel of Mark in the tale of the Gadarene swine (Mark 5, 1–13). On the third day there seem to have been public sacrifices on behalf of the city's welfare; of the fourth, little is known. The fifth comprised the procession to Eleusis, with participants crowned with myrtle. Here we come across Dionysus again, now called Iacchos, whose statue was carried in the procession. Participants raised the cry of, 'Iacchos! Iacchos!' and a spirit of revelry seemed to enliven the group.

In his comedy *The Frogs*, Aristophanes writes in the character of a young man who enjoys sneaking a glimpse at the breasts of young women whose robes have been torn in the boisterous crowd. And as the procession neared Eleusis, the great and the good had to suffer in silence as they passed over a bridge where hooded men gathered to hurl insults at them, doubtless to everyone's delight. Once the procession had reached the sanctuary, dancing and singing went on for those who wished it until after dark.

On the sixth day the participants appear to have rested and made sacrifices to prepare themselves for the initiation ahead. There seems to have been a fast observed, although we do not know for how long. That was broken as darkness fell by drinking a mixture of water, barley and pennyroyal, a species of mint. The participants mimicked Demeter in this action, as she refused to break her fast with wine but requested this kykeon instead. The drink has caused much speculation. Was the barley fermented, or did the pennyroyal have a hallucinatory effect? Whatever may have been the case, the mystes had plenty of time to sleep off the effects, since they did nothing more that day and rested on the seventh day until the evening.

Finally the long period of preparation was over. The participants were by this time dressed in fresh clothes and crowned with ribbons as a sign of consecration to the two goddesses. It appears that the whole night was spent re-enacting Demeter's search for her daughter, the participants holding torches to light their way through the darkness. They seem to have cried out the name Kore, meaning 'maiden'. At each cry, the hierophant (the priest in charge of the Mysteries) would sound a gong to imitate thunder. As the night passed, the participants were taken through the whole range of emotions that Demeter would feel: grief, anger, despair, hope. The Athenian Aristeides says, 'Within this hall the mystics were made to experience the most blood-curdling sensations of horror and the most enthusiastic ecstasies of joy' (Casavis, p.111).

THE EMERGENCE OF LIFE FROM DEATH

All the fragments of writing that survive concerning this part of the initiation make the same point in various ways: that the intention was not to present the initiates with knowledge, but to put them through an experience so that they would absorb the wisdom it contained into their very being. The night was full of drama in order to impress the initiates as much as possible. What, then, was the experience intended to convey? There is no doubt about the answer: it is the experience of death itself. A fragment from Plutarch makes this absolutely clear:

> Thus death and initiation closely correspond; even the words (teleutan and teleisthai) correspond, and so do the things. At first there are wanderings, and toilsome running about in circles and journeys through the dark over uncertain roads and culs de sac; then, just before the end, there are all kinds of terrors, with shivering, trembling, sweating, and utter amazement. After this, a strange and wonderful light meets the wanderer; he is admitted into clean and verdant meadows, where he discerns gentle voices, and choric dances, and the majesty of holy sounds and sacred visions. Here the now fully initiated is free, and walks at liberty ... joining in the revelry. (Grant, p.148)

Once the celebrants had been through such an experience, they would be free of fear. What is more, they would know how to act at the moment of bodily death. The aim of the Eleusinian Mysteries seems, therefore, to be the same as that of the Orphic Mysteries. Firstly the celebrant is taught, in the Lesser Mysteries, that the soul is imprisoned in the body. Then the Greater Mysteries offer the key to awakening the sleeping soul and setting it free.

As the day dawned the initiates must have been exhausted and therefore all the more susceptible to impressions. At this point, the frightening darkness was dispelled by a vision of brilliant light, in which the hierophant appeared. He revealed to the crowd an ear of corn, the gift of Demeter, crying, 'August Brimo has given birth to a holy son, Brimos.' Brimo means strong, so both mother and child are powerful. The names conceal the true identity of the Divinities: Brimo is Persephone and Brimos is Dionysus. The father is Hades. What does this climactic moment mean? It appears to be a revelation of the secret of life emerging from death, just as the initiates have now experienced the joy of eternal life after a night spent in the 'living death' of the sorrowful bodily life.

The initiates also tasted various substances such as grains, pulses and honey in a kind of sacred communion. Although we know that the experience of initiation included the spoken word as well as drama, only a few fragments of the liturgy remain, scattered in quotations throughout the works of various authors. This aspect of the Mysteries must therefore remain for ever unknown. However, the final words of the ceremony are recorded: the hierophant would pronounce the mysterious formula *Knox Om Pax*. The words are said to derive from Egyptian, but the meaning is obscure and it is not even certain that the participants understood them.

All present were now initiates into the Greater Mysteries, known as teletai. They would spend a further day at Eleusis recovering and making sacrifices to their ancestors. Then they would return home, not in an organized manner but just as they pleased. Nothing further was required of them; presumably it was considered that the experience would have been profound enough to change their lives for the better. Ideally, they would have achieved that clear consciousness of which the Dalai Lama speaks and an insight into the true nature of human life and its divine, in-dwelling, spark.

However, there was a final degree of initiation, the epopteia, which could be taken a year later. This seems to have taken the form of a holy light revealing spiritual beings of all kinds, and culminating in a vision of the Queen of the Underworld, Persephone herself. In effect, the initiates would replicate Orpheus' experience of meeting the ruler of the dead while still alive.

OUR HIDDEN TRUTH

In tribal societies around the world we find the figure of the shaman, who alone in his tribe is capable of travelling to and from the spiritual world. The great achievement of the Orphic and Eleusinian Mysteries was to make available this experience to ordinary people. The significance of the Mysteries is profound, for the initiate is thereby assured of continuing, blissful life after death. An understanding of the reality of the soul and its eternal nature can, at the very least, put into perspective the difficulties of daily life. Emotional and physical problems begin to lose their power to rule the initiate, who realizes that life in the body is temporary and that no suffering can affect the soul. Such a realization can allow a sense of freedom and joy to dawn. Some of the initiates may well have had a more profound experience of their own inner divine spark and have decided to devote themselves to the kind of mystical life that would nourish it.

This secret knowledge has never been utterly lost, although it has vanished underground for long periods. After all, it is the truth of our nature, the same today as it was in ancient Greece.

TWO AND A HALF millennia ago, the world was a busy place. Merchants traded across Asia into the Mediterranean and further west, right to the shores of Britain. While some people might never leave their home village, for those who wished to travel there were plenty of opportunities – and along with the merchant caravans and ships went ideas, moving across cultures with astonishing freedom. So it is that the Western Mystery tradition includes wisdom from Eastern cultures, passed down through the ancient Greek philosophers.

> The way up is the way down.
> — Heraclitus

PYTHAGORAS AND HIS PEOPLE

The lore of the Mysteries found its way into philosophy through the work of several of the most influential thinkers of ancient times, men who were – for the very first time in the Western world – inquiring into the physical nature of the cosmos and the spiritual nature of the soul. Their work marks the beginning not only of the physical sciences such as biology, physics and astronomy, but also of the study of the mind and the processes of thought. They used reason and logic to reach their conclusions, yet they also drew on the directly intuited knowledge of the Mysteries: there was no split between these modes of thought. One of the very earliest of these thinkers, Pythagoras, coined the word 'philosopher', which means 'lover of wisdom'.

At this point we need to forget the modern meaning of philosophy. In the ancient world, the word had a far broader meaning than it does today, for wisdom was considered to be found in a number of esoteric disciplines. Pythagoras and his fellow philosophers were not just thinkers but healers, magicians and shamans. They led lives founded on spiritual beliefs, either as hermits or surrounded by devotees. They were regarded with awe and respect. Even Socrates, who is usually presented as a man ruled by reason, was under the power of a guiding spirit and at critical moments in his life found meaning in the Mysteries. Ancient Greece was a far more magical place than we might suspect.

Everything begins with Pythagoras, the first of the historical Western gurus. Although we seem to know quite a lot about him, much of the material is legendary – but even that is significant. Pythagoras was born on the island of Samos, close to what is now the Turkish coast, around 580–570 BCE. Tradition relates that he studied wisdom in Egyptian temples, and that he also visited the temples of Tyre and Byblos, the oldest inhabited city in the world. Hence his knowledge drew on the most ancient sources available. Pythagoras emigrated to Croton in south Italy, where he collected around him a close group of followers who devoted themselves to the secret knowledge he had learned. The Pythagoreans seem to have been very similar to the Orphics; so similar, indeed, that they wrote poems they attributed to Orpheus.

Pythagoras and his disciples seem at first to have inspired a great deal of respect. The citizens of Croton responded well to the Pythagoreans' suggestions that they should live a more moral life, but that happy state of affairs did not last. Eventually a plot was formed against Pythagoras and he fled to Metapontum, where he died at an advanced age. Legend states that he was killed by a thunderbolt, which to the ancient Greeks would have signified a supernatural death. Even during his life, some followers regarded him as an incarnation of the god Apollo. He was apparently very beautiful and his skin had a golden glow; exactly the same is said of the Buddha.

Just as initiates into the Orphic and Eleusinian Mysteries observed a vow of silence, the Pythagoreans too shrouded their beliefs and practices in secrecy. Some things about their way of life, however, we do know. Perhaps the most striking aspect of their society was that women were treated as equals with men – an attitude that was the direct opposite of the prevailing practice in Greece, where women were very much second-

The Pythagoreans lived a life based on friendship, purity of conduct, and reverence for the natural world.

class citizens. Pythagoras' own wife Theano is alleged to have written extensively on mathematics and other subjects.

Friendship was valued so highly that there are stories of Pythagoreans offering their lives in exchange for those of their fellows. Pythagoreans could recognize and hence help each other by using the pentangle as a secret sign. They worshipped and ate together and seem to have held property in common. They ate no meat; a meatless diet was known as 'Pythagorean' until the word 'vegetarian' came into use during the nineteenth century. There was considerable use of music in healing and ritual. Every evening, each Pythagorean would meditate on the events of the day and examine his conscience, vowing to amend any mistakes or unfulfilled duties. The general rule was to follow a middle way in all things, avoiding both excess and asceticism. They are said to have told the truth in all situations, a teaching that Pythagoras brought from Babylon. Their way of life appears to have been a method of taking the Orphic vows of morality further, intensifying their application by living in a group separated from mundane society much as a monastery or convent is.

JOINING THE PYTHAGOREAN CIRCLE

What was it like to join the Pythagoreans? First the aspirant would take a vow of silence, the echemythia, which was valid for three years. He then became a member of an outer circle of Pythagoreans, the 'listeners' or akousmatikoi. At this introductory stage, he would receive basic teachings in morality and be given various riddling verses and mottos upon which to meditate. Among these was the famous order not to eat beans, which has been given various interpretations. Some have thought that as votes were counted with beans, this refers to abstention from party politics. Another, perhaps more likely, interpretation is that certain foods were forbidden for purposes of purification before rituals were carried out in order to have prophetic dreams. The practice of abstaining from certain foods such as onion and garlic before receiving initiations is still in use today in some Eastern traditions.

Akousmatikoi were free to leave the order if they decided, and perhaps that is one of the reasons that the teaching they received was given in obscure forms of which outsiders could make little sense. For example, the Pythagorean saying, 'When the winds blow, worship the sound' is explained by the Neoplatonist philosopher Porphyry (c.305–c.233 BCE) as an exhortation to worship the divine spirit. If the neophyte stayed within the order, he could progress to the next level, that of the mathematikoi. Here he would be taught by Pythagoras himself and the inner meaning of mathematics unfolded.

What did Pythagoras teach? Like Orpheus, he is associated with music, which he based on the study of mathematics. Both these subjects are imbued with mystical meanings. According to Pythagoras, the origin of life lies in ruthmos, rhythm or harmony. What underlies the universe is a limitless void, apeiron. This mysteriously enters the world of form or peiron, and the two combine and recombine in various proportions to create life forms. This is the process called 'harmony'. It is not a random process, for dissimilar elements of being must be brought together in harmonious proportion in order to exist successfully at all. The supreme example of harmony is the perfect precision with which the stars and planets move in the heavens, and this is the 'harmony of the spheres' which Pythagoras was alleged to be able to hear.

All life forms are therefore related, and all are in a constant state of evolving or devolving into more complex or simple forms. The Pythagorean saying, 'Things are number, harmony binds them together' expresses the basic teaching. The universe is a complete whole and a living harmony in which number is not merely a symbol of quantity but produces actual living organisms by the combination of elements. Ultimate reality can thus be expressed in mathematical terms.

We cannot study Pythagoras without mentioning his famous theorem of right-angled triangles. In this context, what is significant about it is that the theorem was known in Babylon and India for centuries before it acquired Pythagoras' name, which only happened some five centuries after his death. Although it is not possible to know when or where Pythagoras came across the theorem, his knowledge of it certainly attests to his mathematical understanding and may support the tradition that he acquired his mystical learning in Asia.

NUMBER SYMBOLISM

A couple of deceptively simple diagrams enshrined Pythagorean number symbolism. The first is the Monad, a circle with a dot at its centre. This symbolizes the single divine principle from which flows all creation. The way in which creation unfolds is shown in the Tetractys, an equilateral triangle with one dot at its peak, two dots below that, then three, then four. The single dot or point of the Monad splits into two, and that represents a one-dimensional surface (a line between two points). A line of three follows, standing for two dimensions (a plane imagined between three points). Finally, the four dots symbolize a three-dimensional four-sided figure or tetrahedron. This progression suggests the process of creation expressed in mathematical terms. The first four numbers are said to represent the music of the spheres, and the ratios are the intervals of basic musical scales: 1:2 is the octave, 2:3 the perfect fifth and 3:4 the perfect fourth. The number of dots in the diagram is ten, a number representing completion, since all numbers above ten are combinations of the first nine numbers.

There are other ways of interpreting the Tetractys. Since it shows the progression of life from the divine unity down to multiple creation, it also holds the key for returning to the Divine. The Pythagoreans did not form their order simply to practise ethical living: if so, there would have been no need for secrecy. They were a religious order and their focus was on living a life expressive of the divinity within. The Tetractys was perhaps their most holy symbol, and their solemn oath was: 'By him who transmitted to our soul the Tetractys, the spring and root of ever-flowing nature.'

That phrase 'ever-flowing nature' gives a clue as to the nature of the Pythagoreans' religious endeavour. They believed that life passed from form to form in a constant process of transmigration. Pythagoras' own teacher Pherecydes is thought to have been the first to teach the soul's immortality and reincarnation through different life forms. According to this doctrine, the soul never dies, but for life after life takes various forms in the way that wax takes the imprint of whatever seal is stamped upon it. It is thus no wonder that the Pythagoreans practised vegetarianism, for animals might harbour the souls of former humans. Pythagoras himself is said to have been able to remember his own past lives, and to have recognized in the barking of a dog the distressed soul of a former human. A Pythagorean saying is, 'All things change, but never cease to be.'

The driving force behind this constant flow of life is simply necessity or cause and effect. And this is where the ethical part of the Pythagorean life comes in. Just like the Orphics, the Pythagoreans felt that the soul must be purified. Whereas the ordinary person would suffer the effects of wrongdoing by being reincarnated into an inferior body, the pure Pythagorean would merit a good reincarnation. But that was not the ultimate purpose. No Pythagorean wished to be trapped in an endless series of rebirths: the aim was mystically to re-ascend the Tetractys to the Monad, there to achieve unity with God. Since all life had come from the Monad, it retained some of the divine quality and could therefore be reunited with it. This is, in effect, the same thinking as that enshrined in the Orphic tale of the death of Dionysus. Such a profound religious belief or insight was to reverberate down the ages in various forms of mysticism, from Gnosticism to the magical order of the Golden Dawn.

PYTHAGOREAN TEACHING

Since the inner practices of the mathematikoi were kept strictly secret, we cannot know what they were. We can, however, speculate that it is likely that the initiations and teachings given to the akousmatikoi served as purifications enabling them to receive more profound, meditative teachings. We know that the Pythagoreans enjoyed a reputation for wisdom, for Plato mentions 'wise men and women' and since the Pythagoreans were the only people to treat women as equals, he must be referring to them.

Music may have played a part in the secret initiations and practices. Pythagoras taught that the universe developed and held together because of harmony. He is said to have discovered the musical scale by hanging strings on a wall and attaching weights at related intervals, then strumming them. In that way, he learned that harmony is mathematically determined – a truth also expressed in the Tetractys. Although this tale is likely to be apocryphal, it does suggest the teaching that Pythagoras developed from his investigations into musical mathematics. Like Orpheus, he was allegedly able to calm both humans and animals at the touch of his lyre. Surely the Pythagoreans used music to harmonize their own beings with the universal chords and rhythms, calming their passions and inspiring their spiritual endeavour. Dance may well have been used in the same way, much as the Sufi turning dance is.

Pythagoras' teacher Pherecydes was an astrologer who is known to have written extensively on the subject, and it is likely that he taught

Pythagoras his knowledge. As we shall see shortly, Plato, who drew heavily on Pythagorean teachings, used astrology in his description of the creation of the universe. We can speculate that Pythagoras also taught his disciples how to use astrology to harmonize themselves with the cosmos, to 'go with the flow' as the modern phrase has it.

The enchanting world of the Pythagoreans was built on harmony, inspirational music, friendship and equality. Although they drew on Orphic lore, there do not appear to have been any dark myths of death and dismemberment involved. That is not to say that initiations did not include frightening elements such as those of both the Orphic and Eleusinian Mysteries. Indeed, it seems that Pythagorean initiations did involve very similar experiences of entry into an unlighted cave, followed by dramatic displays of light and sound. In other words, the initiate was required to go through death in order to be reborn, just as in the earlier traditions. The difference is that he was then part of an order that

Music seems to have been used by the Pythagoreans to calm the emotions and bring peace.

not only offered both physical and emotional support but also regular and graduated teaching. The Pythagoreans were the first such religious community in the Western world, the prototype of all such communities for those who wish truly to devote themselves to the spiritual life.

These peaceable people had an inestimable impact on the development of Western spirituality. Look about and you can still see traces of their presence in the most surprising places. For example, the heraldic insignia for an archbishop's coat of arms includes a green hat embellished with two sets of ten tassels each arranged as a Tetractys. Actual hats can sometimes be seen suspended over archbishops' tombstones. It is doubtful whether Christian archbishops these days are aware of the symbolism, but as we shall see in a later chapter, there have been periods in history when men of the church delved enthusiastically into the mystical Pagan past in order to enrich their spiritual development.

PARMENIDES VISITS THE UNDERWORLD

At the time of Pythagoras, the coast of southern Italy was dotted with Greek colonies. One of these, Elea, was the birthplace of another philosopher, Parmenides. His dates are almost as uncertain as those of Pythagoras, but he seems to have been a younger contemporary, born some time between 540 BCE and 515 BCE.

While Orpheus belongs to the sphere of myth and Pythagoras mostly to that of legend, Parmenides is squarely within history. He did not attract the same kind of mystical stories as Pythagoras; indeed, all we know is the rather sober information that he is said to have come from a wealthy background and to have written laws for Elea. Late sources say that he was 'led to calm' by the Pythagorean Diochaitas, to whom he dedicated a shrine. Parmenides' own work does not appear to draw heavily on Pythagorean thought, although in one aspect it might be said to represent a development. Not much survives of his work: a mere hundred and fifty lines of a poem that may have had three thousand lines. What does survive is not easy reading, either. However, the scholar and mystic Peter Kingsley has elucidated Parmenides' thinking, and the following account is indebted to his insights.

Why is Parmenides important to us? We can answer partly by pointing forward in time to Plato, who valued him so highly that he wrote a dialogue in which Parmenides visits Socrates. Elsewhere in his work Plato always mentioned him with profound respect. Parmenides is said to have been one of the first philosophers to use logic convincingly, thus laying the foundations for Western philosophy right down to the present day. But logic is not our concern, and for the rest of the answer, we have to grapple with some of his poem *The Way of Truth*.

This work is strange to a modern reader and even attracted criticism in ancient times for the obscurity of its language. It falls into three parts. In the first, Parmenides meets a mysterious goddess whose name he does not reveal. She proceeds to instruct him in two ways of knowledge, which form the main body of the poem: the way of truth and the way of opinion. Since the way of opinion is opposed to that of truth, it consists of falsehoods, but Parmenides does not explain why he is devoting many lines of verse to writing untruths. Nor is the section on the way of truth easy to understand. But the introductory section of the poem, in which Parmenides meets the goddess, is cast in the form of a journey that we can immediately relate back to the Mysteries, and that is our clue to its meaning.

Parmenides describes being carried along in a chariot drawn by mares and guided by girls, the 'daughters of the sun'. In the poem as it stands, the reader is dropped straight into this situation with no explanation being offered as to how it came about. What is clear, however, is that the journey Parmenides is taking is a supernatural one, guided by supernatural beings. It could be a dream journey akin to the one described in John Bunyan's Pilgrim's Progress, or it could be an initiation. We learn that the road leads to the 'gates of the paths of Night and Day' and that the daughters of the sun have brought the chariot and mares to Parmenides from the 'house of Night'. Parmenides seems to be travelling along the track of the sun, ending in the Underworld, where the sun vanishes at sunset. That may help explain the namelessness of the goddess who welcomes him there. Persephone, the queen of the Underworld, was one of the dark deities whom it was sometimes safest not to name out loud.

But on this occasion, she is friendly and helpful. Like Orpheus, like the initiates at Eleusis and in the Pythagorean rites, Parmenides has made the journey to the land of the dead while he is still alive. He has travelled the road of souls, 'far from the tread of men' in his zeal for finding truth. It seems that even the revelations of logic require an initiatory experience of descent into the Underworld.

TRUTH AND OPINION

What Parmenides learns from the goddess is broken down into two sections, the 'heart of truth' and the 'opinions of mortals'. Truth is aletheia or 'un-forgetting'. Plato will pick up this definition later, as we shall see. Aletheia is eternal, unchanging and absolute. It can neither be created nor destroyed: it just is. It seems to be the ground of being, perhaps Pythagoras' Monad. Possibly one of the reasons why Parmenides' language is rather obscure is that truth cannot be spoken of but only experienced directly. What Parmenides is talking about is mystical experience, the initiate's direct perception of the reality of the spiritual world underlying the physical one.

In the material world, Pythagoras said, all is change, constant flux. That, says Parmenides, is what makes it utterly unreal in comparison with the eternal reality of unchanging truth. The world of doxa or opinion is one in which things come into being and die in an unending stream. There is nothing stable, nothing on which one can rely, for everything – even thoughts – will disappear. The daily world in which men live is illusory, the inner world of the mind and thought just as much as the outer one. Opinions conflict, change and pass away, whereas truth is incontrovertible, unchanging and everlasting.

Such a view of existence in the physical world is so Eastern that we are forcibly reminded of the way in which learning travelled between Europe and Asia. Although we have no evidence of Eastern sources for Parmenides' ideas, we strongly sense that his world was one in which ideas moved freely and were accepted and incorporated into cultures wherever they were perceived to be valuable.

Up until now, the emphasis of the various initiations we have considered has been on the true nature of the human being – the divine spark and the destiny of the soul. Parmenides himself is clearly an initiate, one who is familiar with the route to the next world. Secure in the Mystery knowledge of his immortality, he turns his attention to the nature of life itself and of truth, thus both deepening and broadening the mystical experience.

The solitary path mapped out by Parmenides, the Eastern sense of illusion, is also present with the philosopher we visit next: Heraclitus.

HERACLITUS THE HERMIT

Heraclitus the Obscure, as he became known, is one of the most enigmatic philosophers of these early times. He was born (possibly around 535–500 BCE) on the coast of Asia in Ephesus, a town under Persian rule. Ephesus was celebrated for the Temple of Artemis, one of the seven wonders of the ancient world. The temple was the centre of a thriving cult of the goddess, and Heraclitus dedicated his written work to the temple, leaving a copy there so that it would be available for all to read.

Once we get a flavour of Heraclitus' personality, that might come to seem a rather barbed act. Heraclitus' view of his fellow citizens' ability to understand anything important was somewhat cynical. His book opens with the unpromising words: 'Of this account (logos) which holds for ever men prove uncomprehending.' The logos is the energy of the universe, and we shall come across it again when we look at Christianity.

The tales that have come down to us about Heraclitus suggest an out-and-out misanthrope. He retired to the mountains outside Ephesus, living in solitude and gathering his food from the plants around him. Allegedly this made him so ill that he was forced to return to the town to seek a cure. When the doctors proved unable to help, he tried a novel and unpleasant treatment by burying himself in cow dung, hoping that the heat would cure him. Unsurprisingly, he died shortly after.

This entertainingly eccentric man lived a life at the opposite pole of the Pythagorean ideal of friendship and co-operation. He seems not to have had any respect for Pythagoras at all, remarking that although he was learned, he lacked sense. But then it seems to have been a habit with Heraclitus to criticize great men from the past, even one so revered as Homer. He claimed that he himself knew everything, and that he had learned it all from enquiring into himself. This statement can seem arrogant, but the phrase 'know thyself' was famous from very ancient times as being the command of the Delphic Oracle. It also seems to have inspired Socrates' theory of knowledge as memory. Heraclitus may have practised a form of meditation, and perhaps the knowledge of which he spoke was that of direct experience. He said: 'If you travel every path you will not find the limits of the soul, so deep is its account.'

Here we encounter for the first time the idea that humans lack nothing necessary in order to achieve their purpose. Heraclitus rejected rituals and initiations: for him, enquiry into the self was enough. He taught that the world proceeds according to a definite plan or law. All the sincere seeker has to do is discover this law and then live in accord with it. But most men sleep-walk through life, living in a world of illusions as in a dream, misled by their senses into believing the world around them to be ultimate reality. Like Pythagoras, Heraclitus taught that the world was in flux: that you cannot step into the same river twice. Everything implies and leads to its opposite. Just as winter turns to summer then war ends in peace. The only refuge for the common man is adherence to the law. For the spiritual enquirer, the same is true – but for him the law is that of the universe itself.

With Parmenides and Heraclitus, we find for the first time hints for the truth-seeker who prefers solitude rather than the support of a communal experience or way of life. Parmenides relives Orpheus' original journey to the Underworld by himself. Heraclitus attempts, albeit unsuccessfully, to retreat altogether from society. Although he does not directly mention the Mysteries, one of his sayings suggests strongly that even his method of enquiry involves a descent into the Underworld. 'The path up and down is one and the same' (Barnes) implies that ascent to the world of the Divine depends upon a descent into darkness. But, as always in Heraclitus, the riddle is left for us to solve. The path seems always to be the same one, whoever describes it and shows the way. What Heraclitus and Parmenides give us is a choice of pursuing the one path as solitary individuals.

VISIONS OF IMMORTALITY

The philosopher Empedocles, who came from Acragas in Sicily, may have known Parmenides, and he was certainly connected with the Pythagoreans. His life is largely unknown, but his death was notorious in the ancient world. The rumour grew that he hurled himself into the volcanic crater of Etna, leaving behind an unusual piece of footwear – one single bronze sandal. It was said that he believed the fire would render him immortal, but as he already claims immortality in one of his poems that seems rather a redundant explanation. During life he seems to have enjoyed great fame and been in demand as a healer; like Christ, he wandered from town to town healing the sick.

Two of Empedocles' philosophical poems, *Purifications* and *On Nature*, survive in fragments, although it is far from clear which lines belong to what poem. The main point of interest for us is that the magical associations of Orpheus surface again with Empedocles. In fact, he quite clearly describes himself not only as an immortal but as a magician who was able to control the weather so as to make crops as fruitful as possible. And, like Orpheus – and Christ – he claims to be able to lead the dead back to the world of the living.

Did Empedocles say how he was able to do this? It seems very likely that he was part of a tradition of handing down esoteric knowledge from teacher to pupil. He addressed his lines about magic to his own pupil Pausinias, promising to hand on all this invaluable learning to him. Presumably Empedocles himself learned from his own teacher. Such a secret history is beyond the reach of the ordinary people who might avail themselves of the Orphic, Eleusinian or Pythagorean Mysteries. However, the figure of the magician is always a singular one; the powers of the Magus are not available to the masses. That is why figures such as shamans and wandering healers such as Parmenides and Empedocles are so important to their societies.

All the currents of thought we have examined so far come together in Empedocles. He revered the Orphic Mysteries and drew from Pythagoreanism and Parmenides. He embraced the idea that the whole phenomenal world is in a state of constant change. He too believed that souls are in bodies as a kind of punishment, doomed to reincarnate throughout the whole of nature until they find the way of escape. The history of medicine has much for which to thank Empedocles, for he was the first to analyse the elements of physical existence into four: fire, air, earth and water. This scheme formed the basis of medical thought for over a millennium. According to Empedocles, two forces, love and strife, rule the universe. Unfortunately, strife has the upper hand in our world, but the initiate can bring body and soul into harmony while the magician can manipulate the energies of love and strife to make changes in the outer world.

By now we can see a clear line of descent from Orpheus onwards. Philosophers from the Asian coast to southern Italy found ways of using, adapting and elaborating on the basic theme of initiation, but the story is always the same. Like Orpheus, several of these philosophers found poetry the ideal medium for expressing the truths they had experienced, and we shall find that to be the case even in the twentieth century. However, the most famous Greek philosopher is not one of these poetic, shamanic figures. He was an urbanite who spent much of his time talking in the marketplace of Athens: his name is Socrates.

SOCRATES AND HIS DAIMON

Although Socrates is such a familiar name that we might feel we are now comfortably within the realm of historical fact, that is not really the case. All we know of Socrates comes from his student Plato's imaginative reconstructions of discussions with and around the philosopher, and these do not pretend to be factually accurate. Plato's Socratic Dialogues have survived in far fuller form than any of the written works we have mentioned so far; indeed, they have formed the basis of Western philosophy. We shall see later that during the Renaissance they were revered as a fount of pure mystical wisdom. Yet the dialogues mark the point at which philosophy – love of wisdom – as understood by the Mystery initiates and magicians separated from philosophy as the use of logic and reason to solve problems or describe the world. Up until then, the two had existed harmoniously. With Socrates and Plato, reason gets the upper hand over experience.

That is not to say that Socrates was not a mystic. It is true that he was famous for refusing initiation into the Eleusinian Mysteries. All the same, he recommended one of his friends to participate in the Mysteries in order to get more out of their philosophical discussions. Socrates himself was celebrated for having his own personal link with the spiritual world, his guiding spirit or daimon. Here it is necessary to point out that although this word became 'demon' in English with a negative Christian meaning, in Greek it merely denotes a spiritual being – what we would call a guardian angel. Socrates' daimon was a protective one that prevented him at critical moments from doing the wrong thing. At times he would stand for hours entranced and motionless, apparently in a state of supernatural possession.

The Dialogues are peppered with allusions to the Mysteries, particularly at crucial points where Plato introduces mythical material rather than a logical line of argument. For instance, the Timaeus gives a creation myth stating that the entire universe is alive, including the stars and planets. God created as many souls as stars. We have eyes in order to see and study the heavens, and intelligence for working out the planetary motions.

What is the purpose of doing that? It is so that we can harmonize our own troubled lives with the serene movements of the intelligent universe. This is almost certainly how and why Pythagoras practised astrology.

Plato's Socrates also believes that souls are reborn. In the Republic, he recounts the story of Er, a man left for dead on a battlefield who experienced the immediate afterlife before returning to consciousness. In his vision he saw souls choosing their future lives, including Orpheus deciding to be a different kind of singer: a swan. The souls were given water from the river of forgetfulness, Lethe, to drink before being reborn. That is a clear allusion to the instructions on the Orphic gold plates for the soul to be careful at which fountain they drink in the afterlife.

PURIFICATION THROUGH LOVE

For Socrates as for the Mystery initiates, the aim of life should be purification and return to the source of being. He even refers to the process as a Mystery: the Mystery of Love. The priestess Diotima explains to Socrates in the Symposium how love is the force enabling mortals to raise their sights ever higher above the material world, until they become utterly absorbed in the immortal and endless ocean of absolute beauty then finally achieve oneness with the Divine. What Diotima describes is a ceaseless ascent from physical to spiritual beauty, an ascent that is not preceded by a descent into the depths of the Underworld. Here is where Socrates and Plato break away from the ancient traditions.

And yet, when Socrates comes to the end of his life and is facing a slow death by hemlock, he wholeheartedly returns to the Orphic and Pythagorean outlook on life. The dialogue Phaedo describes the scene in the prison cell where Socrates' friends gather to say farewell and to listen to him give his last teaching. He discourses on the soul as being imprisoned in the body and remarks on the wisdom of the founders of the Mysteries, since through initiation the soul would go on to a better life.

Here we discover why Socrates refused initiation; it is because he believes that living the philosophical life is just as purifying as undergoing initiation. The philosopher effectually dies to the world before his physical death, since he lives only in the realm of the mind. Socrates' last words, however, open a gulf between him and the earlier initiates, for he orders the sacrifice of a living being, a cock, to Asclepius, the god of healing.

As Socrates' friends close his mouth and eyes, we leave the ancient Greek world. We have seen the first Mysteries and what they meant, how they entered into various philosophical systems and how the experience of initiation became internalized into a mental separation from the world. Although the Mysteries continued to be celebrated, as time passed the

In The Republic, Socrates relates the myth of Er, which tells of souls in the afterlife choosing their future lives before drinking from the river of forgetfulness and being reborn.

knowledge enshrined in them found different paths into the lives of men and women.

CHRISTIAN RAPTURE

THE HOLY MEN of ancient Greece taught their followers the way to eternal happiness through initiation into Mysteries. Starting with the annually recurring mystery of grain and grape, they progressed to the mystery of the love that enraptures the soul. The Eleusinian Mysteries continued to be celebrated for at least five centuries into an era that we think of as a new one: the Christian era. Yet such is the continuity of belief that Christianity itself does not escape the influence of the Mysteries.

> I am the true vine.
> — *Gospel of St John,* 15:1

THE CHRISTIAN MYSTERIES

Christianity was born into a world that encompassed many faiths and cultures. Alexander the Great had pursued his campaign to conquer the world as far as India, spreading the influence of Greek ideas and habits so that they became intertwined with local cultures. About the time that Christ was preaching, another all-conquering empire, that of the Romans, was closing its grip all around the Mediterranean and Aegean seas. Countries as far apart as Britain, North Africa and western Asia were all brought under Rome's dominion. As in the ancient Greek world, trade between countries facilitated the movement of philosophical and religious ideas. In Alexandria, the city founded by and named for Alexander, centres of learning sprang up and the most famous library of the ancient world was founded.

What a melting pot this was! Not only did the Greek gods spread across to Asia, but also it seems some elements of Indian religion made their way westwards. Then there was Zoroastrianism, the religion of the Persians (the Magi), based upon a vision of the world caught in a struggle between good and evil. This faith had a profound influence on both Greek and Roman philosophy. The rites known as the Mithraic Mysteries that were so popular among Roman soldiers appear to have been adapted from, or affected by, Zoroastrianism. Judaism thrived in the Near East, while Plato's Academy in Athens was still in existence and lasted in various forms right up until the Christian emperor Justinian I closed it in 529 CE.

Such a complex picture might suggest that there was no room or need for a new religion, but such was not the case. Christ's teachings were taken up enthusiastically by his followers and propagated with fervour by St Paul, who is credited with forming a creed out of the general principles and beliefs that Christ preached. Christianity, which – like most religions – was based upon ritual, enjoined its adherents to live a moral life and promised them salvation.

But how new was Christianity, and how does Christianity relate to the wisdom that Orpheus and his successors taught? Although it represents a new kind of belief, it shows all kinds of influences from other religious traditions. What we shall examine in particular is the way in which Christianity's roots are firmly planted in the ancient world. Indeed, the hidden wisdom of Pagan Greece finds new life in Christianity, which forms a powerful conduit to carry it into the future. All we have to do is look closely, and we will see that the Mysteries are being celebrated even today, right around the corner from our own homes.

PURIFICATION AND RESURRECTION

The religion founded by Christ is itself presented as a Mystery. In fact, St Paul is particularly fond of the word 'mystery' and uses it more than twenty times in his various writings. He speaks, for example, of the 'mystery, which was kept secret since the world began, but now is made manifest' (*Romans* 16:25–26). This mystery is, of course, only available to Christians – initiates, in effect, who believe in the divinity of Christ as the Son of God. There are direct links here with the traditional Greek Mysteries: St Paul is speaking a language his hearers will understand.

Christ himself might almost seem a familiar figure when we cast our minds back over the mythic and real figures of ancient Greek religion. He is traditionally represented as dressing in white like Orpheus and his teachings have a similar emphasis on peaceable behaviour. Just like Pythagoras, he is a wanderer from town to town, much in demand for his miraculous abilities to heal. Like Empedocles, he can raise the dead and perform other wonders. Indeed, his indifference to worldly goods and security place him in the long line of Platonic philosophers such as Socrates who spurned physical comforts in order to concentrate on the spiritual life and purify their souls. Remember also that Pythagoras was seen as the sun-god Apollo. Christ too is symbolized as the sun, bringing light into a world darkened by sin and evil.

All this is not to say that Christ is a mythical figure. But what we do see is that certain kinds of story constellate around spiritually powerful figures: the ideas of divinity, healing, the power to bring the dead to life. And later, Mystery and initiation. But what is the central aspect of the story of Christ? It is the Easter story of his death and resurrection, which promises all Christians a similar resurrection in the flesh at Judgement Day. Yet even this central mystery brings to mind the fate of Dionysus, torn to shreds and eaten by the Titans, thereby to pass on a spark of divinity to every human being.

PARALLEL THREADS

There are many similar elements in the two stories: too many, in fact, to discuss fully here. Both Dionysus and Christ are destined by their fathers to become 'world rulers'. Enemies threaten each child. The Titans are thrown into the fiery pit of Tartarus, from which image is derived the Christian concept of Hell. Dionysus and Christ are each symbolized by a young animal: Dionysus by a kid, Christ by a lamb. Both are hidden and nurtured in caves, and each is eaten as a sacrificial meal. But here the difference is that it is Christ himself who symbolically breaks the bread and passes the wine to his disciples, pronouncing that these symbolize his body and blood. Thus the rite of the Eucharist is established, and the Catholic Church holds that by the miracle of Transubstantiation what communicants taste is truly Christ's flesh and blood. In effect, they become holy Titans eating and drinking divinity.

Both Christ and Dionysus are intimately associated with wine. Dionysus makes the miracle of wine possible. During his festival in Andros the fountains would run with wine instead of water in commemoration of the first time that happened – at the wedding of Dionysus and Ariadne. Christ, of course, performed the same miracle at the wedding in Cana.

There is even an odd biblical turn of phrase in Euripides' play about Dionysus, The Bacchae. First performed in 403 BCE, it tells of Dionysus' violent revenge against King Pentheus of Thebes, who refuses to recognize his divinity and worship him. Dionysus warns Pentheus not to resist him, not to 'kick against the goad'. Saul of Tarsus (later St Paul) similarly did not recognize Christ as a divinity and busied himself persecuting Christians with enthusiasm. On the road to Damascus he was blinded by a great light, and heard Christ's voice observing that 'it is hard for thee to kick against the pricks' (*Acts* 9:5). The similarity of the two occasions, four centuries apart, is striking.

Christ himself was actually identified as the 'real' Dionysus, announcing to his disciples at the Last Supper, 'I am the true vine, and my Father is the husbandman,' (*John* 15:1). His development of the metaphor seems to suggest that the old vine, Dionysus, is dead: only Christ can now offer the blessing of spiritual intoxication.

But Dionysus is not the only sacrificial god whom Christ resembles. His priest Orpheus also taught a new gospel of one supreme god; he suffered a violent death at the hands of a mob, after (according to early accounts) successfully raising his wife from the dead. He too continued to exist after his physical death. Early Christians were well aware of the parallels between the two figures – so much so, that the depictions of Orpheus simply passed into Christian iconography. There are many pictures of Christ as the Good Shepherd, from Italy to Jerusalem, that are indistinguishable from depictions of Orpheus. Typically, Christ will be shown wearing a Phrygian cap and holding a lyre, surrounded by animals. Early Christian writers such as Clement of Alexandria explained that Christ outdid Orpheus since he tamed the wildest animal of all, the human being. Other pictures of Christ carrying a lamb derive from ancient Greek statues of Hermes Kriophorus ('the ram-carrier'). We might also note in this context that according to myth, Hermes carried a ram around a city to cure the inhabitants of plague. He was also the guide of the dead, who could enter and leave the realm of Hades at will.

THE LIGHT IN THE DARKNESS

Clearly the early images of Christ owe much to the Mysteries, and according to the Gospels, Christ understood that his teaching needed to address the Mysteries as well. Not only the Orphic Mysteries but also the Eleusinian are alluded to in the Gospels. For example, Christ preaches the parable of the Sower who sows his grain on both good and bad ground. His ordinary audience would have appreciated the agricultural imagery, but initiates among them would also have recognized the symbol of the growing corn. Indeed, Christ explicitly tells his own disciples that the parable is intended for them as initiates: he explains, 'Unto you it is given to know the mystery of the kingdom of God,' (*Mark* 4:11). His other listeners, who do not have the key to understanding, 'see, and [do] not perceive ... hear, and [do] not understand' (*Mark* 4:12). Here Christ is clearly stating his role as a master of esoteric knowledge that can be passed on only to initiates.

Christ explains that the corn seed is the Word, the logos. According to the Gospel of St John, Christ himself is the logos, who was in the beginning with God and who entered the world as a great light shining in the darkness. He is Heraclitus' logos, the principle upon which the universe is founded. But he is also the bread, the resurrected grain of Demeter and Persephone, which he breaks and distributes at the Last Supper. Like Persephone, he descends to Hell after his death on the cross, to rise again purified and triumphant.

As Christianity developed, its rites took on other similarities with the Mysteries. There was purification through baptism, after which the initiate was allowed to partake of the Eucharist and take into his or her body the divine spark. Christianity developed its own Mysteries: the seven sacraments of baptism, confirmation, the Eucharist, holy orders, confession, the anointing of the sick and marriage. Initiates were sworn to secrecy on these Mysteries. The significance of the Christian Mysteries was that at critical points of life, the initiate would come into direct contact with God. In every way, then, Christianity followed the form and the purpose of the ancient Mysteries. Everyone who participates in the Eucharist today tastes the grain and the wine that go right back to Demeter and Dionysus, thus testifying to the power of the Orphic and Eleusinian Mysteries to survive across millennia.

Yet Christianity is a religion distinct from the Mysteries. For one thing, it is not a cyclical religion: souls do not reincarnate, history does not turn with the year; time marches on relentlessly towards the Final Judgement when the dead shall arise and reassume their flesh. This doctrine of the resurrection of the body is very different from the ancient view that placed all the emphasis on the soul's welfare and counted the body as an uncomfortable prison. And although Christ descends to harrow Hell, his followers do not get a glimpse of the afterlife as the Eleusinian initiates did. The movement away from descent to the world of the dead and towards a one-way ascent to the light that we saw beginning with Plato continues with Christianity. Indeed, the philosopher Nietzsche called Christianity Platonism for the masses. Instead of offering a psychological experience of death, Christ tells his disciples that by losing their lives through physical death they will be saved. Hence the tradition of gruesome martyrdoms begins. Death becomes merely an act that ends life on earth and precipitates one to heaven – rather than an experience during life that assures one of heaven.

MYSTICAL VISIONS

The Christian experience of other worlds during life thus echoes Socrates' ecstatic vision of ultimate beauty. The first to mention such an experience – in effect, the first Christian mystic – is St Paul. He began life as a Pharisee of Roman extraction, and during his early years he hated the Christians with such gusto that he confesses to active persecution of them. Paul may have been a younger contemporary of Christ, although there is no record of them having met. Paul's conversion to Christianity is sudden and highly dramatic. On the way to Damascus where he intends arresting more Christians, he is felled by a brilliant light that blinds him. A voice identifying itself as Christ laments Paul's cruelty. Paul is then led to Damascus where after three days Ananias, a local Christian, miraculously cures his blindness. Thereafter Paul is baptized and becomes an indefatigable, if controversial, apologist for Christ. He travels in Asia and Greece spreading the word, the first Christian missionary. At Ephesus, the birthplace of Heraclitus, he causes uproar by preaching against idols: a risky thing to do in the town famous for one of the seven wonders of the ancient world, the statue of Artemis. Eventually Paul seems to have died in Rome.

Paul's mystical experience is as much of a rebirth as initiates experienced in the Mysteries. Before his conversion, Paul was named Saul, but he took the new name during his first missionary journey. Paul was born anew, full of faith in the resurrection and the grace of God. The birth takes place in light rather than the darkness of a temple or cave. And yet, what is the effect of this light? It is to blind Paul, who then spends three days alone in his private darkness, neither eating nor drinking. After all, it seems that this Christian initiation is not so different from the Eleusinian, Orphic or Pythagorean ones, albeit a solitary individual accomplishes it as an unexpected experience rather than participating in an organized mass ritual.

Perhaps as a result of his rebirth through light and darkness, Paul also enjoyed a mystical flight to heaven. He states that he was 'caught up to the third heaven' (*2 Corinthians* 12:2). There, in paradise, he heard 'unspeakable words, which it is not lawful for a man to utter' (*2 Corinthians* 12:3). He cannot say whether he was in or out of the body at the time. Such an ecstatic journey not only parallels those of the ancient world but also preserves the Mystery tradition of secrecy. However, Paul follows in Socrates' footsteps by locating the place of ecstasy as upwards, in the light. And what does he mean by the 'third' heaven? It is a spiritual heaven, the abode of God. The first heaven is the immediate atmosphere, the air; the second, the visible universe around us. These are both physical realities and as such, imperfect: only the third heaven is perfect and holy.

The Christian view of the world as it develops through Paul and onwards no longer regards the world of nature as sacred. Gone is the idea that all life is holy, that souls can move from body to body. Dionysus' sacred vine and Demeter's grain are no longer blessed – until, that is, the priest miraculously changes them to Christ's blood and flesh. All holiness is now located in heaven, all evil in hell which gapes like a dungeon beneath the earth. Only humankind can, if blessed by the sacraments and God's grace, become sanctified. This is the Christian Mystery, and this is where it departs most profoundly from the ancient Mysteries.

But the power of ancient ideas is too great to be extinguished, and it reasserts itself in strange yet suggestive ways. One of Paul's most celebrated converts was Dionysius the Areopagite, a judge from the Athenian court. Even though Dionysius was a common enough name in the Greek world at that time, the irony of him being so named for Dionysus is apparent. What is more, we shall meet Dionysius again in a later chapter, for mystical texts appeared under his name in the sixth century CE – although they are certainly not by him. These short texts offer Christian ideas about the mystic path to God in Platonist terms, for Plato too lived on, his ideas not only surviving alongside the new and ever-growing faith of Christianity but developing and strengthening as fresh interpretations delved deeper into their meaning.

THE NEW PLATONISTS

In the complex religious world of the early centuries following the Crucifixion, the boundary between Platonism and Christianity was in many places amazingly permeable. The two systems had in common a sense of exile from a heavenly home, and while in some ways they varied on techniques for recovering that home, in others they agreed.

Plato's influence on the thought of the ancient world is incalculable. While Pythagoreans and the Mysteries continued a secretive existence during this period, what Plato had done was to bring the eternal questions of life into the open for individual meditation and debate. And, just as Christ's teachings developed into the organized system of beliefs enshrined in Christianity, so Plato's thought was elaborated and given various applications by subsequent thinkers. Some of these were men born to wealthy families who could afford to devote themselves to philosophy, but some were humble labourers who gave up their livelihoods in order to become teachers.

Such a man was Ammonius Saccus (c.175–242), a porter in Alexandria. Although both his parents were Christian, Ammonius taught Plato and Aristotle. His life is obscure, but his fame rests upon a single achievement: that he taught the great Neoplatonist Plotinus (c.204–270). In a sense, Plotinus stands between worlds: he inherits the whole rich past of Greek mystical experience and he stretches his hand over the future with his emphasis on individual thought. Born in Egypt, he studied in Alexandria under several teachers before he found Ammonius. Wishing also to learn from Persian and Indian mystics, Plotinus joined an army headed for Persia. However, the campaign was a disaster and he had to find his way back alone. We do not know how much he was able to absorb during his travels, but we can be sure that this enthusiast for philosophy garnered some wisdom along the way. Plotinus then spent most of the rest of his life in Rome, surrounded by his students. Plotinus' writings were collected and published posthumously by his devoted pupil Porphyry, who learned – with considerable difficulty – to read his almost unintelligible handwriting and to decipher his odd turns of phrase.

What interests us most about Plotinus' voluminous works? There are several aspects. One is that Plotinus was a true mystic. Like Socrates and St Paul, he experienced raptures during which he was lifted up into the presence of a marvellous beauty, 'acquiring identity with the divine' and feeling that this was his own true self. Plotinus writes that he had this experience many times, although he does not explain how or under what circumstances the rapture occurred. Did he perform some ritual or meditation to bring it about, or did it happen spontaneously? Porphyry, who wrote a biography of Plotinus, tells that he used meditation and the method outlined in the speech given by Socrates in the Symposium. That is, Plotinus would begin by contemplating some beautiful person or thing and gradually raise his thoughts to abstract ideas of beauty until the absolute beauty of divinity enraptured him. Porphyry reveals that Plotinus did not feel at home in his body, and that his final words on his deathbed were of returning his inner divine spark to the absolute Divine.

So we find that in both the Christian and Neoplatonic traditions, individual experience begins to predominate over group ritual. The individual strives for a personal union with the Divine, and what was once a social (though secret) experience becomes a private matter. Porphyry himself declares that he too achieved union with the Divine just once, when he was 68 years old. And he says that Plotinus received divine guidance, for when he was thinking or acting along the wrong lines, the gods would pour down light upon him to illuminate the right way.

THE GUIDING SPIRIT

Plotinus opens paths forward for us too, for with him we come across the elaboration of a concept we met when considering Socrates: that of the guiding spirit or daimon. While it seemed an unusual thing for Socrates to be advised by a spirit, a mark of his unique nature, Plotinus states that every person is similarly blessed. The daimon's nature is matched to the individual. Porphyry tells us that Plotinus' one is exceptional. An Egyptian priest visiting Rome offers to evoke Plotinus' daimon. They go to the temple of Isis, where the priest successfully conjures the spirit – but it turns out to be no mere spirit but an actual god. So terrified is the priest's assistant that he accidentally strangles two birds he is holding (possibly for sacrifice), and the vision vanishes. Plotinus, Porphyry assures us, kept himself focused on that in-dwelling presence which lifted him above the general run of humankind.

According to Plotinus, our guiding spirit is a kind of higher self. Every time we are reborn, we take on a body and life appropriate to our former habits and inclinations. Thus those who have lived for the senses may be reborn as animals, whereas those who live a life of the spirit will be born as humans in touch with a higher reality. If such a person continues to strive spiritually they will develop accordingly and their inner guide will similarly evolve. God, says Plotinus, is within us all, albeit most of us are unaware of his presence. What Plotinus and Porphyry seem to experience in their raptures is a temporary glimpse of life as it is for the perfected person who is in direct touch with the One, Plotinus' term for God. Once this has been experienced, Plotinus believed that the desire for sensual pleasures would fade away and with it, the tendency to be reborn. Eventually the philosopher-sage would achieve liberation from the ceaseless round of birth and death – just as Pythagoras taught.

Such was the open nature of religious practice at this time that Christianity had no difficulty in adopting the daimon in the guise of the guardian angel. In this context it is interesting to note that Plotinus wrote a lengthy critical essay against the Christian Gnostic sect, castigating them for seeing the world as an evil place. For the Neoplatonists, as for the earlier mystics we have described, life is holy once it is seen from a spiritual point of view.

THE LAW OF SYMPATHY

The Neoplatonic world-view as Plotinus elaborates it is of a universe that is totally alive and sentient, from the stars downwards. Everything is linked in a vast network of influence, so that one can read the stars as a kind of language descriptive of events on earth. That is astrology, the discipline for which Plato said man had been given eyes. Every soul, says Plotinus, descends from a particular star with which it has affinities. Not only that, but each star throws out a line of influence that reaches down through people, animals, plants and even stones. Thus the universe is organized in a hierarchy of connections, great chains of being. This is known as the law of sympathy or correspondence – and here is the point where magic begins to seep into the picture. We have already heard of Empedocles raising the dead and controlling the weather. Now Plotinus begins to give us clues as to how magic may work. If you correctly identify which parts of creation belong together, you may tweak the line of influence and catch the attention of the power ruling the line.

In fact, according to Plotinus all of life is an enchantment. Once seen under the light of the principle of sympathy, it becomes clear that everyone acts in accordance with what fascinates them, as if under compulsion. Only the true philosopher is not susceptible to enchantment, for his meditations draw him to the sublime, one to the exclusion of all other influences. Hence philosophical union with the One is the only real liberation, and that experience of union caused Plotinus to wonder how it is that the soul comes to be in the body at all. A mythical explanation, like the story of Dionysus and the Titans, is not enough for him. He examines Heraclitus, Empedocles, Pythagoras and Plato looking for answers but finds them obscure. Eventually he realizes that just as the guardian daimon looks after the human being, so the human soul has some responsibility for the next link down in the chain of being: the material world. If the soul dives into matt er and leaves again as swiftly, it returns easily to its godlike state. But if it lingers, it becomes as if stuck in mud and then the fascination of sensual pleasure works its magic to keep the soul in place.

Plotinus uses the familiar Pythagorean image of the body as a prison, from which it is possible to escape by turning one's back on the material world and climbing, rung by rung, the ladder of the chain of being right up to the realm of pure divinity. But for Plotinus, the soul's proper duty is to enter the material realm in order to care for it and to experience life in full. Here we have for the first time the idea of the world as a school, in which the soul learns its own nature. This is the fullest explanation we have so far seen of the paradox of human life and destiny.

THE ENCHANTED WORLD

Plotinus lived at a time when Christianity was about to be made the official religion of the Roman Empire. All the same, his Pagan thought proved immensely influential on Christianity. We have already seen that the Christian writer Dionysius the Areopagite adopts the Neoplatonist view of a hierarchically organized universe. He is responsible for the vision of nine orders of angels, described in his *Celestial Hierarchies*. However, much closer to Plotinus in time is one of the great Church fathers, St Augustine (c.354–430). His father was a Pagan but his mother was Christian, so Augustine grew up with a variety of viewpoints. Having tried Zoroastrianism, he turned to Neoplatonism to satisfy his urgent spiritual yearning, and there he found a description of divinity that satisfied him. Augustine was inspired by the thought of a purely spiritual God and of the soul's return to its source, based on meditation and self-knowledge. However, he moved on to Christianity in search of a personal relationship with God, which he felt the intercession of Christ provided.

While Augustine felt it necessary to make clear choices about his faith, other Christians managed to compromise. Such was Synesius of Cyrene (c.373–414), who studied under one of the rare female Neoplatonist teachers, Hypatia of Alexandria. This civilized and sophisticated man devoted himself as much as possible to a leisurely life of literature and hunting, writing on fascinating subjects such as alchemy and dreams. Synesius was also a highly able military strategist, showed an informed interest in astronomy and wrote amusingly on going bald. When he was requested (by popular demand) to take up a Christian bishopric, he agreed only reluctantly and made several stipulations. One was that he could remain married, and he also insisted on retaining his independent Pagan beliefs on such tricky points of doctrine as the immortality of the soul, the resurrection of the flesh and Judgement Day. Amazingly, he was allowed these concessions.

Such were the early Neoplatonists: mystics who focused on their inner life stood alongside practical men who lived worldly lives. These two aspects come together in the practice of magic. As we have seen, Plotinus views magic as a compulsive force that traps people into desire and illusion. Only the true philosopher is free from magic, a point that Porphyry proves in one of his stories. According to him, a jealous fellow

Miracle-worker Empedocles

philosopher, Olympius, used spells to try to hurt Plotinus – but Plotinus, being focused upon union with the One, could not be harmed and the spells rebounded on Olympius, convulsing him with agony.

Plotinus' view of magic did not deter his successors from becoming increasingly interested in the subject. Wonder-tales abounded about later Neoplatonists, just as they did about Pythagoras and Christ. Iamblichus of Chalcis (c.245–325), who lived in Syria but exerted a huge influence throughout the Hellenic world, was known as a miracle-worker, despite his own strenuous denials. He is important to us principally because he laid great stress on the divinity inherent in matter. This paves the way for magic, and indeed Iamblichus seems to have advocated ritualistic practices as a means of achieving unity with the Divine in addition to, or instead of, meditation. He wrote much about Pythagoras and revered him above all other philosophers.

A PROPHET AND MAGICIAN

It is with Proclus (412–485) that we move fully into the magical world. The greatest late Neoplatonist, Proclus was credited with control of the weather just as Empedocles was. His biographer Marinus claims that he was able to save Attica from a catastrophic drought, and that he could also predict earthquakes. Proclus was also gifted with the ability to intercede with the Divinity of healing, Asclepius, and so save lives. He believed himself to be the reincarnation of a Pythagorean called Nichomachus, and his dreams told him that he was in the chain of being emanating from the god Hermes, which includes the planet Mercury. Such was Proclus' understanding of philosophy that he considered differences of religion unimportant. Calling himself the hierophant of the world, he felt universally responsible and he practised the rites of many religions with equal respect.

Marinus' account of Proclus describes a man of almost daunting austerity and virtue, yet with a gentle and kindly character illumined by the highest inspiration. Proclus lived a life full of prophetic dreams, of signs and wonders and appearances by various gods. We seem to be back in the ancient Greek world, where the Eleusinian initiates could meet Persephone face to face.

What's more, Proclus outlines the way in which those less favoured than himself may contact the gods – through magic. In his short work *De Sacrificio* he describes how every person, animal, plant and stone belongs to one or another gods. He uses Plotinus' idea of the chain of being to explain how each god (or divine principle) has a rich mixture of qualities. As the god's influence filters down through the world of nature, these qualities become separated into less ample containers. The astute magician can gather these together – stones, herbs, animals and so on – so that the divine qualities are united again and a channel is opened up for the pure influence or presence of the god to flow down into him. This practice is known as theurgy: 'divine work.'

Proclus describes the lotus, opening its petals to the sun in the morning and closing them at night. He likens this to the movements of a mouth in prayer, and suggests that if our ears were attuned to fine vibrations we could hear the lotus praying. 'The earth is full of gods,' says Proclus: everything that lives is blessed with divine essence to a greater or lesser degree. His theurgy is based upon the meditation on Love in the Symposium – the very meditation that Plotinus used to unite himself with the One. The theurgist can similarly raise himself to spiritual heights by ascending the chain of being that connects the material things of this earth to their spiritual superiors. Someone wanting to contact the power of the sun, for example, would work with gold, sunflowers, cockerels, all of which are sacred to the sun.

Proclus also writes of the power opposite to that of sympathy, upon which this magic is based. By invoking antipathy, the theurgist can cleanse himself of spiritual impurities. The salt tang of seawater, for example, is used for purification. Marinus writes that Proclus himself used to bathe monthly in the sea. Proclus also mentions substances that are effective singly for particular purposes, such as laurel or diamond for a protective amulet.

The main aim of theurgy – to unite with or draw down divine powers – is similar to Plotinus' mystical endeavours, but it's clear from Proclus' description of making amulets or using spurge-flax to manifest a spirit that we are in the realm of magic. This aspect of Neoplatonism will echo onwards right through into medieval times and through the Renaissance, even affecting the development of science. Somehow the urge to escape from the magical lure of the world becomes combined with an irresistible desire to learn how to use the enchantment all around us. We can see that this has been so right back to the myth of Orpheus charming the animals with his song. Now the mystical philosophers have given the clues that will enable generations of magicians and alchemists to follow in their tracks.

PERSIAN MAGIC

HOW DID THE MYSTICAL knowledge enshrined in Neoplatonism find its way into the West? The story is strange and its route circuitous. Plato's school, the Academy, survived in various forms from its founding date of around 385 BCE until its final reincarnation as a centre of Neoplatonism, which the Christian Emperor of Rome in the East, Justinian I, shut down in 529 CE. By this point Christianity had grown powerful by virtue of being the official religion of Rome and did not tolerate rival paths to mystical experience. However, fortunately for the Neoplatonists, the situation in different parts of the world was more accommodating.

> Now, if thou wilt, follow me, come with me toward him.
> — Avicenna, *The Story of the Birds*

ORACLES AND FIRE

By the early sixth century CE the members of the Academy were no longer solely Greek; in fact, several hailed from Syria. The mixing of cultures throughout the Roman Empire and the East proved to be the saving grace of Neoplatonism. Packing up their scrolls of philosophy and mysticism, the last Academy members sought sanctuary with the king of the Persian Empire, Chosroes I. Some seem to have settled in the Persian capital city, Ctesiphon, while others chose to live in the Turkish town of Harran. Here they pursued their studies and practices, protected by a guarantee of their personal safety agreed between the Byzantine and Persian Empires. Although the philosophers who chose Ctesiphon as their home did not stay long, they did participate in the work of translating into Persian the texts they carried with them. Later, Chosroes sent to India and China for learned men who brought their ancient cultural wisdom to Persia to mingle with the rich currents already flowing there.

The religion of the Persians was Zoroastrianism. This ancient belief system focuses on the contrast between forces of light and darkness in the universe. Zoroastrians align themselves with the all-powerful deity of goodness, helping to maintain the sacred order of existence by positive and moral actions. St Augustine spent some time as a convinced Zoroastrian before he turned to Neoplatonism and finally Christianity. And here we enter into the Neoplatonic world to find writings that were attributed to Zoroaster and were profoundly influential on the Western development of the hidden knowledge. The Chaldean Oracles comprise a collection of obscure sentences and fragments from a poem describing the origins of the universe and the path the soul must take in order to free itself from the confines of matter. This should sound familiar, since it has a basis in Orphism. It is thought that the Oracles were received mystically by Julian the Theurgist, who served in the Roman army. The Neoplatonists revered the Oracles as offering profound insights into reality; in fact, so highly were they regarded that they have survived right up until the present.

The complex world of the Chaldean Oracles can be summed up in the idea of the ascent of the soul. Trapped in matter, it is the business of the soul to return to its spiritual home with the transcendent deity by rising up through the planetary spheres, shedding as it goes all accretions of impurity both physical and spiritual. As in Zoroastrianism, the deity is symbolized by fire: 'All things have been generated from One Fire' (Majercik, p.53). The soul rises throughout the spheres with the help of angels, 'by making the soul bright with fire' (Majercik, p.95).

So obscure and difficult are these fragments that they constitute true mysteries. What we see here is the beginning of a great mingling of religions, with texts being produced that owe ideas and inspiration not just to one religion but to several. The Oracles, though considered Zoroastrian, are also Neoplatonic and include elements of Egyptian religion. In the heady Hellenistic world of the Near and Middle East, wisdom could be drawn from all and any available sources.

At about the same time the Oracles were written, another of the most esoterically influential texts of all times was compiled. Unlike the Oracles, which survived largely through being quoted by Neoplatonic authors in their works, this piece of ancient wisdom largely dropped out of sight until it was dramatically rediscovered during the Renaissance. In fact, as we go on with our story we will increasingly feel that the passing of time is not as simple as we might think from looking at a clock. Time seems to open and close like a door, alternately revealing and hiding the knowledge accumulated by ancient cultures.

This writing claimed to be a revelation of ancient Egyptian wisdom, handed down from the god Thoth to his disciple Tat. The language is Greek and Thoth is referred to as Hermes Trismegistus – thrice-great Hermes. The collection of texts has come to be known as the *Corpus Hermeticum* or *Hermetica*. We shall look more closely at the Corpus in the following chapter, but for now it is important to know that one of the texts tells the thrilling story of how Tat achieves a purification of his entire being

The mystical text Corpus Hermeticum was said to offer the wisdom of the Egyptian god Thoth.

and finds that he is now one with the entire universe. This secret doctrine is complemented by other texts dealing with magic and alchemy in an intoxicating brew of arcane mysteries. We can get a sense of how mixed and mingled with esoteric studies all religions became at this period when we discover that Zoroaster was considered to have invented astrology. It seems that wisdom takes a new turn and leans towards practical magic, the use of astrology to harmonize the self with the world, and the use of alchemy to pursue perfection.

THE LAND OF HAROUN AL-RASCHID

Here we enter the world of the *Arabian Nights*. First the Persians and then the new force of Islam laid great emphasis on learning, and although that learning encompassed medicine and science, such disciplines were not discrete from areas such as astrology and magic. Indeed, medicine depended upon astrological timing and alchemy was considered to be science. We should remember that 'science' merely means 'knowledge'.

Chosroes I revitalized a great centre of learning, the Academy of Gundishapur, with the wisdom brought by the Neoplatonic philosophers and the sages from India and China. In 638 CE, Islamic Arab armies conquered the Persians and power passed from the Zoroastrian culture to the Islamic one. However, the Islamic caliphs valued learning just as highly as their predecessors, and founded a sister academy in Baghdad, known as the House of Wisdom. Scholars from all cultures were welcomed at these academies and works from East and West were translated into Arabic. At one time, the romantic figure of Haroun al-Raschid, the hero of many of the magical *Arabian Nights* tales, was thought to have founded the House of Wisdom. What is certain is that he influenced a golden age of culture that flourished during successive reigns of caliphs for about a century of intensive learning and discovery. It is said that Caliph Al Ma'moun paid for Greek texts with their weight in gold. The House of Wisdom survived until 1258, when invading Mongols destroyed it, flinging the texts into the river Tigris. But the light of truth is not easily extinguished, and by that time the knowledge enshrined in the House of Wisdom had spread elsewhere – even, as we shall shortly see, into England.

During the era of the House of Wisdom, knowledge was still being passed on from teacher to pupil by word of mouth and several great personalities made their mark upon the times. These men were Renaissance men long before the term had been invented: polymaths who pioneered work in philosophy, medicine, astronomy, mathematics, music and many other disciplines. The best of them were open-minded to any learning that served their search for truth. Such a one was Al-Kindi (c.801–873), a Muslim Arab who won for himself the title of 'The Arab Philosopher'.

WISDOM FROM INDIA

Al-Kindi was profoundly involved in the translation of ancient Greek texts into Arabic, and inevitably became fascinated by their wisdom. He took on the Neoplatonist view that the whole universe is alive and that the planets are divine beings who obey the will of God. As for the soul, it is immortal. Al-Kindi described the life of the soul after death as one of purgation and purification. He did not believe in Hell but imagined the earth as a bridge between worlds, from which the soul rises to the sphere of the planet Mercury to be purified. From there it continues to the sphere of the stars, then to the highest heavens, and the World of Reason. One final ordeal awaits: the 'crossing of the shade' before the soul reaches its home and destination: the Light of the Lord.

At this moment of fruition, the soul becomes omniscient. Looking down on the world, it will feel attracted to some particular task. The Lord will assign it the appropriate duty, a small part in running the universe in an orderly way. This new development in Plato's idea of ascent reflects the other influences on Al-Kindi's thought: those of the Orient. He was known to have mastered Indian as well as Greek ideas, and here he seems to be thinking of the Mahayana Buddhist concept of the bodhisattva. Anyone can aspire to be a bodhisattva. Once he or she has achieved full perfection and liberation from the round of birth and death, the bodhisattva chooses not to enter nirvana but to return to the suffering world in order to guide others towards the light.

So now we have compassion entering the picture. No longer is the question that of individual achievement of rapture; instead, the bliss of final peace is sacrificed in order to help others. And in many other ways, Al-Kindi enriches Greek ideas with Indian wisdom. Again and again he stresses the virtue of non-attachment, an idea that is important to the Hindu faith and central to Buddhism – but he points to Socrates as the

Medieval Islamic philosopher Al-Kindi translated the works of Plato and Aristotle from Greek into Arabic, allowing for a wider audience for their ideas.

perfect example of the non-attached man, citing his claim that he was always happy because he owned nothing that could cause him grief by being lost. Happiness, says Al-Kindi, is to be found in rejoicing over another's good fortune: that sort of joy cannot be disappointed.

True happiness is not dependent on external circumstances, but is an inner accomplishment: a slave is free if he knows how to be contented, while a free man may be enslaved by greed. Al-Kindi writes a great deal about the need for self-mastery and discipline of the passions of desire and hatred: these values too echo the psychological insights of Indian philosophy. For Al-Kindi, adherence to the truth and the practice of generosity are all-important. Yet he is more than just a moralist. He writes that philosophy is 'the practice of death ... the separation of the soul from the body' (Atiyeh, p.19).

Here we might remember that mysterious area of shade that the soul has to cross before reaching the final Light of the Lord. The Neoplatonic idea of a steady and inexorable ascent towards the light of perfection has here been taken back, in some sense, towards the ancient Eleusinian recognition of a need for an ordeal of darkness before the soul can reach its true home. Even the Lord of Light is not the clear and mystically joyous vision of beauty that Plotinus experienced. Rather, He is ineffable, beyond all description. Al-Kindi here reflects ideas put forward in the works attributed to Dionysius the Areopagite.

Al-Kindi was an expert astrologer, applying in a practical sense his mystical ideas of the planets being alive and divine. From his point of view, if a man was to live a properly moral life in harmony with the universe, he had to know how to align his actions to the movements of the planets, the agents of God's will. Astrology thus becomes a mystical tool that the philosopher uses in his pursuit of truth.

THE LIGHT OF GOD

One of the greatest of the Arabic masters was the Persian philosopher and mystic Avicenna (c.980–1037). He was a prodigy from an early age, full of self-confidence and unwilling to accept criticism. Like Al-Kindi, his knowledge covered an incredibly broad range of subjects and he is revered as the father of modern medicine. Yet he was also a mystical philosopher who taught by means of allegory.

Avicenna lived during a time of considerable upheaval and in his constant search for a patron encountered difficulties that even landed him in prison. This experience he turned to the good by experimenting with sensory deprivation, a kind of meditation that has parallels in Indian techniques. The subject imagines himself floating in a void, unable even to feel his own body. Nothing but consciousness remains. Such a technique strips away all the accretions of the material world, leaving only an awareness of the soul, the essence of the self. It is significant that Avicenna attempted this experiment in conditions of darkness and imprisonment, far from the comforts of ordinary existence. There are echoes here both of the Eleusinian experience and of Al-Kindi's remark about the slave who is secretly free.

A system of mysticism is clearly set out in Avicenna's later works. He proposes the idea of a lodestar of knowledge that draws the soul. First the mystic develops the intention to reach his goal, and uses spiritual discipline to leave behind the passions of life and to soften his character so that he can become totally absorbed in devotion. Soon he begins to experience brilliant flashes of the light of God, which induce ecstasy. With perseverance, these mystic moments become increasingly frequent until flames of light permanently envelop him. At this point he gains an angelic companion to guide him. The awareness of companionship too increases, until the mystic eventually sees God in his own soul. He has arrived at the goal of his journey – the journey that so many have taken before him.

Here too there is a moment of darkness, since the mystic who has achieved initiation into the spiritual world is then able to leave his own body – Plato's and Al-Kindi's 'death', Orpheus' journey to the Underworld. Just as for Socrates, so for Avicenna the world is a prison and his true home is elsewhere. And Avicenna speaks of the journey to the light in terms that are already familiar to us from the Orphic Mysteries. In a mystical story called *The Tale of Hayy*, we are invited to travel to the world of light with an angelic companion. This world lies in the Orient, where the sun rises; at this point we are reminded of Parmenides' initiatory journey to just that place. And, as we are instructed in the Orphic gold plates, we must pass through a region of darkness before arriving at a spring where we are to drink and bathe. Now fully purified, we are fit to meet the Divinity.

In opposition to the spiritual Orient lies the material Occident: here, where the light of the sun is extinguished, is a hell of hot and muddy seas, salt deserts and men trapped in the bodies of animals. Such too is the vision of Orphic regions of purgatory. It is as if in this tale we have returned to the source of all mystical knowledge.

Despite this, and despite his use of alchemical procedures in his medical innovations, historians like to present Avicenna and the other great Arabic and Persian thinkers as rationalists. Yet, at the end of his mystical Tale of the Birds, Avicenna includes a paragraph satirizing those who will dismiss such a spiritual story as the ramblings of a man who has temporarily lost his mind. It is perfectly clear that he realizes that proclaiming spiritual truths in the market place invites ridicule. True wisdom is only for the few, who are initiated by their own desire to reject the superficialities of daily life in favour of profound spiritual illumination.

Avicenna revolutionized medicine, and he had profound spiritual experiences.

THE ALCHEMICAL QUEST

Avicenna was known in his lifetime as a magician, and for him and other philosophers of the time, Plato too was a magician and alchemist. To understand why, we must remind ourselves that philosophy was not the practice of rational argument it is today, but a practical discipline of body as well as mind. In the *Phaedo*, Plato reports Socrates as speaking of purification through separating the soul from the body. Avicenna and his contemporaries understood this to refer not simply to an inner discipline but also to a chemical process of purifying physical substances in order to draw out their essential power. Hence Avicenna's interest in alchemical procedures for the production of medicines: he wanted to find cures that used the purest substances possible.

As with philosophy, so with alchemy – the Persians and Arabs drew on a rich variety of sources from Egypt to China. Perhaps one of the most influential was Bolos of Mende, a town on the Nile delta. He flourished in the second century BCE and was a Neopythagorean, working with numbers in a mystic sense. Bolos seems to have made one of the earliest attempts to create gold by precipitation of the philosophers' stone. But this wasn't simply a physical procedure, nor did Bolos dream of achieving riches. The scholar Peter Kingsley reveals that the alchemy that was passed on to the Persian and Arab masters of knowledge concealed the secrets of initiation as practised by Empedocles, Parmenides and Pythagoras. Hence the recognition of Plato as an alchemist, for he had inherited the same secrets.

WISDOM FLOWS WEST

The knowledge enshrined in alchemy was refined and developed by the Persians and Arabs, particularly by Jabir ibn-Hayyan (c.721–815). He was known in the West as Geber and it is from his name that we derive the word 'gibberish', for he wrote in a code almost impossible to penetrate. Jabir was active at the legendary court of Haroun al-Raschid, and in that romantic setting he pursued alchemical studies based on number symbolism and the attempt to create life itself. He looked back to Pythagoras, Socrates and Hermes Trismegistus as founders of the art, and it is clear that he practised it as a spiritual discipline. Jabir taught that the alchemist was required to purify himself before starting the work by retreating to the desert and performing elaborate prayer rituals. Even then, he would succeed only if he submitted himself entirely to God's will.

Jabir was immensely influential on European alchemy, and the way in which his works reached the West forms part of the story of the flow of wisdom across cultures. We can consider the Persians and Arabs the sole keepers of the flames of hidden knowledge about 300–1100 CE, but during this time the course of history began carrying esoteric texts back westward. This happened in several ways. The Islamic empire of the Arabs had reached as far as Spain, where fabulous traces of their sophisticated civilization still stand, such as the Alhambra at Granada and the Mezquita mosque in Córdoba; and from the end of the eleventh century a series of crusades lasted for almost two centuries, bringing Western Christians into contact as well as conflict with Eastern cultures. At the same time, Christian kingdoms within Spain began to squeeze out their Islamic rivals. This long struggle was to culminate in 1492, when the Catholic king and queen Ferdinand and Isabella expelled not only the last Muslims but the Jews too.

Not all Western Christians were hostile towards other faiths, and learned men appreciated the subtleties and depth of Eastern learning. What's more, scholars were astonished to find that some of the Platonic wisdom, lost in the West, had been preserved in Arabic. Great feats of translation were performed, and doors opened in Europe to an inner world of secrets that led to the development of arcane arts such as alchemy and astrology.

A fine example of the movement of the ancient wisdom back to the West is summed up in the life of Abraham ibn Ezra (c.1092–1167). He was one of the amazing polymaths of that period, learned in philosophy, medicine and literature. In his life, he was most famous for bringing Jewish learning to the Christians of Europe, through Biblical commentaries and grammars. Some considered him to hint at knowledge of the Kabbalah in his works. But to later generations he became known first and foremost as a skilled astrologer who had a deep influence on Western practitioners.

Ibn Ezra led a wandering life. Born under Muslim rule in Spain, he was forced to leave the country to escape persecution. His subsequent travels indicate a man eager to learn: he moved from north Africa to

Egypt, then to Israel; from there to Italy, up through France and then to England. Here he stayed in Oxford and London, before returning to France. The place of his death remains a mystery.

Everywhere he went, ibn Ezra was accompanied by the precious Arabic works he had safely removed in his flight from Spain. He also composed original works, such as the book on religious philosophy known as the Foundation of Awe that he composed for a Jewish friend in London. His thought was imbued with Neoplatonism, so he can hardly be called orthodox. His two great works on astrology – The Beginning of Wisdom and The Book of Reasons – draw on the first-century works of the Egyptian Greek astrologer Ptolemy. Ibn Ezra devotes the first sentence of The Beginning of Wisdom to the warning that in order to succeed in his art, the astrologer must live in awe of God, turn away from worldly things and calm himself with meditation. These are exactly the kind of instructions that alchemists were given: the disciplines are alike in being basically spiritual. The astrologer who learns how the heavens work gains insight into the divine mind, just as the alchemist does by practising chemistry. Both find that the outer world mirrors the inner: in the words of Hermes Trismegistus, 'as above, so below'.

THE ALCHEMICAL BISHOP

The influx of wisdom from the Arab world was thrilling to the educated men of the time – and the most educated men of all were connected with the church. Monasteries were repositories of rare texts and clerics taught at universities. Foremost among these, and famed in his day as one of the most learned men of his time, is Albertus Magnus (c.1200–1280).

Albertus, who was born in Bavaria, enjoyed a long and illustrious career, rising steadily throughout the Dominican order to positions of power and influence. But he preferred a life of study and devoted himself to learning, achieving a remarkably encyclopaedic knowledge of subjects reminiscent of the greatest Persian and Arab thinkers. He was responsible for great feats of translation, making available in Latin (the medieval lingua franca) a vast range of learning from Greek and Arabic sources. Albertus had a huge curiosity about the natural world and, seemingly, a sense of humour; he owned a snake that one day got drunk and flopped around the cloisters, much to the amusement of the monks.

His Christian faith did not prevent Albertus from practising astrology and – allegedly – alchemy. Indeed, astrology is central to his beliefs. Like practitioners before him in the East, he thought that the study of astrology was an aid in performing the will of God. By understanding the course of the planets, an individual could follow the currents of the time, in harmony with the universe. Albertus also advocated electional astrology, the art of choosing a propitious time for action. Here too his reasoning was that we should heed the signs that God has placed in the heavens. Albertus' book on astrology, the Speculum Astronomiae, enjoyed immense success and influence for centuries after his death.

By Albertus' time, the mystical writings of Dionysius the Areopagite had reached the West. They were regarded with awe, since they were believed to be the work of St Paul's first convert. Albertus accepted their philosophy whole-heartedly, writing commentaries about the *via negativa* – the mystic path that insists that God is ultimately beyond and above our knowledge. Yet Albertus also managed to convey the idea that faith can give us a direct knowledge of God, just as wine is known by taste rather than description. Indeed, he reaches right back to Diotima's speech on the Mysteries of Love in Plato's *Symposium* to offer his own *via positiva* – an ascent towards the 'highest delight' of contemplating God.

Although Albertus thought of God as being transcendently unknowable, at the same time he believed that God fills the world and everything in it. Such a belief opens up the study of every subject as sacred scripture, including alchemy, astrology and even biology. And, since all creation is essentially divine, it is logical that it has occult and mystical qualities. Albertus wrote about the mystical properties of precious stones and even animals. Such was Albertus' fame that many books were later written and circulated in his name, but even though we cannot be sure of his authorship such works as *The Book of Secrets*, detailing the magical properties of stones, herbs and animals, gives a clear idea of how magical ideas developed during the medieval period and later. However, in such magic books we are a long, long way from the pure spiritual aims of the theurgists. For example, we read that eating a still-beating weasel's heart confers the power of prophecy. There is no hint here of contacting the gods – just a rather sinister use of nature for personal gain.

Even when the magical practitioner performed rituals to summon angels (or demons if ill was intended), the aim was to bind these superior beings to work the magician's will. A rich literature of ritual and ceremonial magic grew up and flourished throughout the medieval period, accompanied by texts on astrology, alchemy and the making of images. Even though magic focused on gaining material advantages rather than on spiritual development, it had a surprisingly pious slant. Almost all texts emphasize that the magician needs to prepare himself by fasting and washing. Many prayers familiar from church services would be used as incantations, and holy water was considered particularly powerful. Some rituals even required the making and use of a crucifix. In many ways, privately performed magical rituals derived from religious ritual. After all, the church itself employed a kind of magic to alter the substance of bread and wine in the Eucharist.

THE ART OF DYING

The ancient Orphic idea of preparing for the afterlife by experiencing death before actually dying seems to have disappeared in the medieval period. Even the influx of mystical Arabic texts on the theme did not keep it alive. That is not to say that the subject of death was avoided during this period – far from it. Graveyards surrounded every church and inside the churches elaborate tombstones were decorated with skeletons. Songs reminded listeners of death's imminence. In the fourteenth century the horror of the Black Death probably halved the population of Europe, and coincided with the Hundred Years' War. No wonder mystical death was blotted out of memory when physical death was such a ubiquitous presence.

So, instead of mysterious tales of the philosophical death, we find death manuals in wide circulation. These books were intended to be read to the dying as guides to the next world. They thus form a direct parallel to the Orphic gold plates, although their instructions are much more elaborate. The difference is that the dying person has not had the advantage of an initiation, so he is facing death for the first time. He is recommended to commend himself into the care of his guardian angel – and here we remember the daimon who guided Socrates and the angel who called to Avicenna to follow him through the planetary spheres, across the Shade to the Divine Light. The tradition of mystical death does still survive, although in a very modified form.

THE PHILOSOPHERS' CATHEDRAL

The church undeniably dominated medieval life, finding its way into magic, the art of dying and even into alchemy. But the opposite process may be true too: that alchemy found its way into the church. This is the period of the great Gothic cathedrals of Europe, 'sermons in stone' with soaring architecture designed to awe and inspire. They are mystical buildings, loaded with symbolism that draws on some of the writings we have considered. For example, in the twelfth century Abbot Suger designed the first and one of the greatest of the cathedrals, St Denis, just outside Paris (now encompassed by a northern suburb of the city). 'Denis' is the French version of Dionysius, the very Dionysius the Areopagite who wrote of God in Neoplatonic style. Abbot Suger based his designs on Dionysius' description of divine light, creating great stained-glass windows to flood the interior with a mystical brilliance that would seem like a visionary answer to the worshippers' prayers, and he enshrined the supposed relics of Dionysius in the cathedral.

Albertus Magnus influenced the decoration of Strasbourg Cathedral, but there may be even more arcane secrets carved on the faces of other cathedrals. According to a mysterious twentieth-century alchemist, Fulcanelli, the elaborate symbols on Notre Dame and other cathedrals lay out the secret processes of alchemy for all to see. Fulcanelli (a pseudonym) wrote two books on alchemical architecture, the manuscripts of which he entrusted to his sole disciple, Eugène Canseliet. Like all alchemists, he preserved total secrecy and both received and passed on his knowledge orally. Canseliet claimed that Fulcanelli received the mystic initiation of the 'Gift of God' and achieved the philosophers' stone, which Canseliet himself saw in action. At this moment of supreme achievement, Fulcanelli vanished, leaving Canseliet to oversee the publication of his books. He reappeared briefly 27 years later, in 1953, looking younger than before.

Such a tale is typical of many stories about alchemists but it holds a peculiar fascination for having happened so recently. There has naturally been much speculation about Fulcanelli's true identity. That must remain for ever mysterious, but we do still have his books. The first, Le Mystère des Cathédrales, describes in riddling language the alchemical symbolism used on such buildings as Notre Dame in Paris. According to Fulcanelli, notre dame – Our Lady – refers not only to the Virgin but also back in time to Sophia (wisdom) and even to Demeter. He points out that some depictions of the Virgin show her gown decorated with vines and ears of corn. So here we have symbols of Eleusis and the Dionysian Mysteries of Orpheus. Fulcanelli also notes that a carved figure on Notre Dame wears a Phrygian cap, which is the distinctive mark of initiation into the Eleusinian Mysteries.

Certainly some of the carvings around the base of Notre Dame are very strange indeed and although some appear to show biblical subjects, who is to say that those stories too did not have esoteric meanings? If Fulcanelli is right, then the Eleusinian Mysteries in alchemical disguise are there for us to see and ponder, right in the heart of Paris.

DANTE THE INITIATE

The great Italian poet Dante Alighieri (c.1265–1321) was born just over a century after the cornerstone of Notre Dame was laid. During that time cathedrals were springing up all over Europe, fraught with symbolic rose windows, labyrinths and sculpture. Magicians and alchemists practised both within and beyond the church. Dante, however, chose literature to express his mystical vision. The great event of his life happened very early, when at the age of nine he encountered his beloved Beatrice, whom he likened to an angel. From that moment on he devoted himself to her in a mystical sense, since their actual meetings were rare and fleeting. Indeed, he married another woman, Gemma Donati.

Sadly, Beatrice died young in 1290, after which Dante devoted himself to philosophy. By 1308 Dante had begun his masterpiece, *The Divine Comedy*, which occupied him until shortly before his death. This vast work describes a vision of the afterlife. Dante is led through the circles of Hell, up to Purgatory and finally – triumphantly – through the planetary spheres until he becomes absorbed in an experience of Divine Light. The Roman poet Virgil guides Dante through Hell and Purgatory, but his beloved Beatrice takes him up towards Paradise. The work expands on Dante's basic belief that love 'is the heartbeat of the whole universe' (Ficino, p.12).

So Dante takes this ancient, Pagan idea of ascent through the spheres and gives it a Christian gloss. Just like the Orphic initiates, he is instructed to drink at a stream before ascending from Purgatory to the celestial

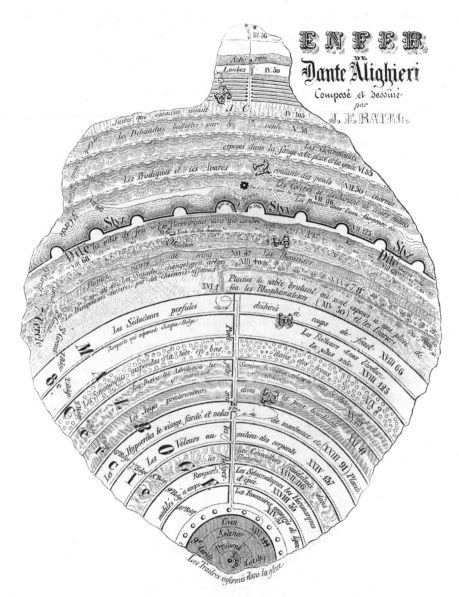

Dante described in poetry his journey through the spiritual realms of Hell and Heaven.

spheres. This purifies him so that he is fit for the ascent. Each planetary sphere is a heaven in itself, and in the fourth – that of the Sun, representing wisdom – he comes across Albertus Magnus the alchemist.

The final vision that Dante achieves is the goal of every mystic: to separate the soul from the body before death so that it can become one with God and the universe. Is Dante's description of Divine Light merely literary, or is it based on personal experience? He describes himself as one who 'had come from time to the eternal' and we may speculate that the intensity of his love for Beatrice was for him an initiatory experience that, coupled with his philosophical studies, led him to the mystic death after which, it seems, he had nothing more to achieve; shortly after finishing his great work, he died. Did he join his beloved Beatrice in the afterlife? We may speculate that just as Diotima promised in Plato's *Symposium*, love led him to the realization of his soul's desire.

We have come a long way from the early Persian and Arabic philosophers to Dante, so let us close the circle by mentioning that some scholars have detected the influence of Islamic mysticism in *The Divine Comedy*. Certainly Avicenna would have recognized Dante's cosmic pilgrimage – but then so would Plotinus, Plato and Orpheus himself. The only difference is that Dante turned his mystical experience into one of the greatest and most inspirational poems of all time.

RENAISSANCE MAGUS

SO FAR IN OUR STORY the hidden knowledge from ancient eras has ebbed and flowed through time and cultures, eventually concealing itself during the medieval period in such arcane disciplines as alchemy and magic. But the current has flowed on, and we now reach a point at which it bursts forth into the light in such a way that it will reverberate right up to our own times. This is the pivotal point in our tale: the Renaissance.

Through love of God you will one day
re-create yourselves as gods.
— Marsilio Ficino, *Letters*, Book 7

INTO THE LIGHT

The Renaissance is a high point in Western culture, focused in fifteenth-century Italy – particularly in Florence – but then rippling out across Europe. In two or three charmed generations an extraordinary assembly of geniuses painted, sculpted and wrote poetry as never before. They broke away from the formal styles of medieval tradition, creating a new and vibrant realism that forms the foundation for all art that follows. Even such renegade twentieth-century artists as Francis Bacon revered and emulated Renaissance artists. Michelangelo, Raphael and Leonardo all worked at this time.

At the same time, a great influx of learning produced 'the Renaissance man', who boasted knowledge in a whole range of areas from poetry to science. The way we are educated today owes much to Renaissance ideals.

But where did Renaissance knowledge originate? Although this is a matter for scholarly debate, we can say in simple terms that ancient wisdom from Greece and Rome reentered the world, inspiring a new enthusiasm for the ideals of the classical civilizations.

Amazingly, that ancient wisdom was nothing other than the hidden knowledge that Plato so cryptically enshrined in his writings. It was the initiatory rites of Orpheus and Eleusis that thrilled the Renaissance philosophers and reinvigorated art, politics and knowledge of the natural world. The Renaissance sees all the available ancient wisdom gathered safely up to be passed on to future generations – indeed, to us. It is as if the Renaissance were a door swinging open, revealing to the future the distant past, and this momentous turning point in the history of the secret wisdom happens because of just one man: Marsilio Ficino. This small, modest man who was plagued all his life by ill health achieved a profound understanding of what the ancient philosophers were doing, and brought their wisdom to life for his contemporaries and for us.

THE FIRST RENAISSANCE MAN

Ficino was born just outside Florence in 1433. His father was a doctor whose patients included the great Cosimo de' Medici, the effectual ruler of the Florentine republic. Ficino's mother Alessandra had the gift of second sight, and Ficino too had visions at crucial points in his life. From his father he learned medicine, which he practised for his friends all his life, and through his father he also came to the attention of Cosimo, who recognized in the young man a talent for languages and translation that he determined to use to the full.

The great impulse towards rediscovering the ancient wisdom was born thanks to the Council of Florence in 1438–9. Cosimo himself offered to host the council, the intention of which was to unite the Western and Eastern branches of the Church. The Byzantine emperor John VIII Paleologus himself attended, accompanied by a group of scholars from Greece. Among them was Gemistus Pletho, a controversial figure whose reading of Plato had caused him to revert to worship of the ancient Greek gods. Pletho brought with him texts by Plato that had been lost to the Western world, and he taught the Platonic wisdom to groups of interested Florentines. Although the Council was unsuccessful, it thus fulfilled an invaluable function. Cosimo bought or was given many ancient texts and he collected more as time passed.

There was one drawback: the texts were in Greek, whereas Latin was the lingua franca of the educated man of the time. But in 1459 another

Marsilio Ficino, a key Renaissance figure, brought back to light Plato's teachings.

Byzantine scholar, John Argyropoulos, came to Florence, where he taught the Greek language as well as philosophy. Ficino learned Greek from him, and in 1462 Cosimo entrusted to Ficino his text of the complete works of Plato for translation. But before Ficino could make much headway, a monk arrived from Macedonia bringing an almost complete copy of the *Corpus Hermeticum*. Although some of the Corpus had survived the medieval period, nothing so complete had been known in the West. Here, felt Cosimo, was the true ancient wisdom, a mystic knowledge that predated Plato and hailed from the most ancient of civilizations: Egypt.

Cosimo was an old man by now and wanted to be enlightened before he died. He instantly ordered Ficino to stop translating Plato and get to work on the Hermetic texts instead, so Ficino immersed himself in the ancient wisdom from both sources. And that was just the beginning. He went on to translate the Neoplatonists too: Plotinus, Porphyry, Iamblichus. Then the Orphic Hymns and Fragments took Ficino right back in time to the earliest sources of mystical knowledge. Although he worked at incredible speed, his translations were so accurate that they still command respect. More importantly, Ficino revered and understood the ancient authors: he entered fully into their mystical vision of the world. So profoundly did he feel the living presence of the wise men of the past that he revived Plotinus' habit of celebrating Plato's birthday with a banquet – a tradition that had not been observed for twelve centuries.

But Ficino did not simply revive the ancient knowledge: he strove to make it relevant for his contemporaries. He himself was an ordained priest, and his great aim in life was to synthesize Pagan Greek wisdom with Christianity. The Church had even lost over time the doctrine of the immortality of the soul, which Ficino revived. Not only did he translate Dionysius the Areopagite, but he also felt a profound interest in St Paul and his raptures. Indeed Ficino was working on a commentary on St Paul when he died.

Despite leading a quiet, scholarly life, Ficino had a profound influence not only in Florence and Italy but all over Europe. Despite being a melancholy and retiring man, he enjoyed a vast circle of friends and acquaintances, many of whom were the most famous and talented men of their day in politics and culture. He was friend and tutor to Lorenzo de' Medici, Cosimo's grandson, known as the Magnificent. He did not scruple to give advice to rulers and popes alike, though the King of Hungary asked in vain that Ficino should come to grace his court with his incomparable learning. It is extraordinary that Ficino's reputation rested entirely on the ancient hidden wisdom.

Ficino was a true Renaissance man, for as well as bringing to life the ancient wisdom he was also a highly skilled astrologer and he practised a new kind of magic – one that was holistic, natural, safe and deeply psychological. Indeed, much of Ficino's thought is startlingly modern and relevant. Let us delve into some of the various aspects of his world.

THE GOLDEN CHAIN

Ficino derived from Gemistus Pletho the idea that a common wisdom, a universal truth, had been handed down in various guises throughout the ages, and that he and his contemporaries had inherited it. Later this would be called the perennial philosophy. He looked back across all the mystics we have studied so far and saw that their lives and thought formed an unbroken chain of succession; the aurea catena or golden chain. Zoroaster, Hermes Trismegistus, Orpheus, Pythagoras, Plato and Plotinus are the main links. Other philosophers derive their knowledge from these masters or elaborate on their innate wisdom.

As Ficino himself had inherited this wisdom, he felt that he himself had become a link in the chain, bound by God's Providence to pass on the hidden knowledge. He himself seems to have experienced the rapture that Paul and Plotinus alike enjoyed, being swept up through love into unity with the Divine:

> What strange fire consumes me now? ... Oh joy beyond understanding! I am now out of my mind, but not mindless, because I am beyond mind ... Now I expand in every direction and overflow but am not dispersed, because God, the unity of unities, brings me to myself, because he makes me live with himself. (Ficino, pp.38–9)

Such words echo and may even have been inspired by the Corpus Hermeticum, in which Hermes Trismegistus initiates his pupil Tat by an experience of unity with the cosmos. Clearly Ficino felt himself to be an initiate of the Mysteries. What's more, he gathered around himself men who had the same fascination with the ancient wisdom and who were also eager for initiation. Ficino often mentions in his letters his Platonic Academy. According to him Cosimo first had the inspiration to revive Plato's Academy of philosophy, and chose Ficino as its head. He gave Ficino a villa at Careggi, near Florence, where he could study, write and hold meetings of the Academy.

Much speculation as to the nature of this Academy has taken place over recent years, even to the point where its existence has been doubted. But whatever form the Academy took, it is clear that Ficino was at the centre of a circle of men who were learned in mystical and occult knowledge, and that they looked to him as their teacher. The great poet and humanist Angelo Poliziano wrote with enthusiasm of the thrilling effect of listening to Ficino discourse vividly on astrology, medicine and philosophy. So profoundly inspiring was Ficino that Poliziano would return home feeling eager to write poetry and enjoy the ecstasy of music.

THE NEW ORPHEUS

Ficino himself was famous for his music. He suffered all his life from a melancholy temperament, and would cheer himself by singing and playing on a lyre. But this was no ordinary singing: on the contrary, Ficino's music was magical. He believed himself to have revived the actual music of Orpheus, and his friends joined him in that belief, referring to him as the 'new Orpheus'. They spoke and wrote of his power to charm by song and music, using it as a therapy for anyone in need. So highly did Ficino value this style of singing that he claimed its revival as one of the great achievements of his age, implying that he was far from being the only person to practise it.

Can we then discover what this new Orpheus sang? We can certainly learn what significance Orphic music had for Ficino. He read in Plotinus' *Enneads* a beautiful image of the relationship of souls to the Divine. Souls turning towards God, says Plotinus, are like a choir facing the choirmaster. Once they turn away, they cannot follow his directions, but facing him they contribute to a glorious universal harmony. This harmony is, of course, the music of the spheres. Moreover, Ficino says that that musical harmony vibrates right throughout creation, from the spheres down to the individual. So Orphic singing is a way of harmonizing oneself with the universe, of expressing one's place in it according to the Divine Will. And on a lighter note, it aids the memory, since an enjoyable activity is easily remembered.

The content of Ficino's Orphic songs falls into at least two categories. Ficino translated the *Orphic Hymns* in 1462, but he never published them. He wrote to one of his correspondents that he did not want to be accused of reviving the worship of Pagan gods, and that he followed Pythagoras' example in concealing divine things from profane eyes. Each hymn invokes a Greek deity and is accompanied by directions for herbs and spices to be burnt as it is sung: they certainly are Pagan prayers. The Church kept a sharp eye on unorthodox practices, and Ficino had to tread carefully to keep out of trouble. We know though through his friends' descriptions that Ficino sang the hymns privately and when he was with members of the Academy. So highly did his friends value Ficino's singing that one sent him a costume of Scythian boots and a fur coat so that he could dress up as Orpheus!

Why did Ficino consider the hymns to be such a powerful source of magic? His reasoning stems from Plato's *Phaedrus*, where Plato outlines four kinds of divine madness: poetic and musical (Orphic), religious or ritual, prophetic and amorous. All these paths lead to the Divine – we have already seen that Diotima outlined for Socrates the path of love. But with his Orphic music, Ficino goes right back to the source of the secret wisdom. His friend Poliziano testifies to this, claiming Ficino as a more powerful magician than Orpheus, for he has succeeded in bringing the ancient knowledge back to life. Such strong magic could only be suitable for those who had prepared themselves for it by living a philosophical life.

THE HEALING HOROSCOPE

However, Ficino also composed music for everyday healing purposes. As well as Orphic hymns, he laid great store by astrologically composed music and song. In the third of his *Three Books on Life*, he sets out rules for making songs in styles that will evoke the various planets, together with instructions for suitable times for singing them. For example, someone going through a difficult period of life might benefit from evoking the warmth and light of the sun. To do so, they would sing a song in a cheerful yet dignified manner, ideally at a time when the sun was strong, such as midday. Ficino himself composed suitable astrological music for his friends that would have a good effect on their souls and minds. When doing so, he first studied their horoscopes, for a song would only be effective if it reflected the planetary influences therein. Harmony as a principle exists not only in music: the horoscope must harmonize with the song in order to bring the person into line with his horoscope – then he will be in harmony with the divine order of the cosmos.

According to Ficino, song is like a living animal with a soul of its own. It is therefore particularly beneficial to listeners' souls. But what of the body? That can be calmed and healed by dance – Orphic dance. Ficino looked to a statement in Plato's *Timaeus* that there is 'only one way to look after anything and that is to give it its proper food and motions. And the motions in us that are akin to the divine are the thoughts and revolutions of the universe' (Lee, p.119). The universe, being made of spheres, moves in a circular way so that is the right way to dance. Ficino recommends performing a kind of Sufi dervish whirling, as much as one can without getting dizzy and in as large a circle as possible. Ideally one should be outdoors, so that the beneficial influences of the air and sky can pour down and be wound into one's system by the whirling movement.

We can imagine Ficino in the grounds at his villa, whirling under the night sky while meditating upon the planets and absorbing their friendly rays. The dance can be used in a specifically astrological way: for example, someone whose horoscope is under the harsh influence of Mars or Saturn could find out when Venus would be strong in the sky and dance to draw down her gentle rays. It is a holistic therapy, combining a physical exercise that also induces a meditative calm while attracting (according to Ficino's belief) helpful cosmic influences.

PRACTICAL MAGIC

Ficino straddled the ancient and modern worlds, gathering up all the threads of secret wisdom from the past and seeing the underlying unity. Although some of the Mysteries, such as those of Eleusis, could not be revived, Ficino found new ways of celebrating them – and his outlook and methods are near enough to us in time and culture, and modern enough in understanding, to be useful to us today.

For Ficino, trained in medical studies, was a supremely practical man. He wrote three self-help manuals: one for scholars, one for the elderly and one for anyone who wants to align themselves with the beauty and order of the cosmos in order to live a happy and healthy life. He called it *On Obtaining Life from the Heavens*. Let us recall here Plotinus' view of the cosmos as alive and interconnected, with each star and planet raining down influences that penetrate all being right down to the rocks and earth; Ficino, who translated and revered Plotinus, held this view and based a whole system of magical therapy upon it.

In order to be well, both physically and spiritually, we need to be in harmony with the universal influences. For Ficino, this begins with a study of an individual's horoscope to discover which planet the person belongs to in particular. Say the horoscope shows a strong Mercury; the person will have a guardian angel or daimon who is part of the mercurial chain of being, and he will benefit by practising such pursuits as writing or playing games which belong to Mercury. He should also sing mercurial songs, light and airy in style. Herbs that fall under Mercury will be good for him, likewise foods. He will enjoy the company of mercurial people and feel good when dressed in mercurial colours such as light blue.

Ficino's prescriptions can become complicated because they are so all-embracing, but they can also be very simple. The key concept is that of harmonizing all the powers symbolized by the planets. So, for example, someone labouring under the dour influence of Saturn (like Ficino himself) needs to balance it by invoking the light and splendour of the sun. He can do this simply by walking in the sunshine, allowing the rays to penetrate his body and the light to cheer his mind.

MAGICAL PRACTICES

That is, to our mind, simple psychology – but when Ficino goes further we enter the realm of magical practices. A much more powerful way of drawing down solar power is to combine items from all levels of the solar chain of being: something belonging to a solar kind of man; some part (such as the heart or blood) of a solar animal, plant matter, spices, a suitable gem and the metal gold. Once all these things are gathered together, they must be ground into a medicine or unguent for spreading on the body – but only at an appropriate time, when the sun is astrologically powerful.

Ficino lists animals, plants, gems and spices that belong to the sun, noting also that solar daimons can be encountered in the forms of cockerels and lions. The world of spiritual beings is as real for Ficino as the visible world, for spirits belong in the cosmic hierarchy and indeed are profoundly important in linking the material world with the higher realms of the planets and the Divine.

If this sounds familiar, it is because we encountered such ideas in Proclus – in fact, we have Ficino to thank for having found and translated (in 1489) Proclus' short work on magic *De Sacrificio* and for reintroducing the idea of the harmony of the world. Now magic no longer relied on garbled Church prayers and invocations of angels or bad spirits. Instead it had a philosophical basis in the Law of Correspondences: magic now made logical sense. Ficino's influence in this respect alone is incalculable, as we shall see in later chapters.

Indeed, Ficino restored the original purpose of magic. We know that Proclus worked his magic in order to contact the gods, to raise himself to their divine level. Can we say that Ficino too is practising theurgy? If we think back to the medieval magicians, using their craft to gain money or skill, or even to harm an enemy, then we can definitely say yes. Ficino's aim is always, without exception, a pure one of bringing the practitioner into alignment with the cosmic order according to the Divine Will. This may be performed on many levels. The highest is not for everyone, and that is why Ficino kept his Orphic Hymns for a select circle of acquaintances. But On Obtaining Life from the Heavens starts from basics and leads the reader through a number of ways to improve their physical and spiritual health so that they will not only enjoy life more but also live more harmoniously in the material world.

LIVE LONG AND PROSPER

Ficino describes a seven-step programme to achieve health of mind and body. First, one should use suitable images, perhaps engraved on a ring or other jewellery to be worn on the body. Then come medicines, compounded from suitable substances and at the astrologically correct time according to the rules given above. Next, pleasant odours are to be used as a kind of aromatherapy. The fourth therapy is musical: the astrologically based song mentioned earlier, accompanying the whirling Orphic dancing.

These therapies benefit the body. Next come three ways of improving one's mental outlook and emotional health. The imagination is to be nourished, perhaps through the reading of poetry or viewing of art. Good conversation, attendance at lectures and serious reading all exercise the reason. The highest rung on this ladder of holistic health is contemplation: what we would call meditation. It might come as a surprise to find that Ficino was aware of the range of benefits deriving from meditation. Although he does not give his sources, it may be speculated that he learnt from the Arabic authors he so often quotes (such as Avicenna), who had contact with Indian and Chinese mystics.

Ficino suggests setting aside a room for meditation, preferably in a quiet part of the house, where the meditator should spend as much time as possible and even spend his nights. The focus for meditation should be a visual image of the entire universe, either painted or constructed so as to show the planetary spheres and coloured in gold, green and sapphire blue (the colours of the three benefic or friendly planets: the Sun, Venus and Jupiter). Meditation upon this image will, says Ficino, help to keep the meditator calm and focused even when he emerges from the room into the hustle and bustle of daily life. And slowly but inevitably, he will begin to realize that he contains the entire heavens within his soul. All the planetary forces are there, for man is related to the universe as microcosm is to macrocosm.

But what about the need to make a living? Himself an impoverished priest who was constantly searching for a better income on which to survive and – later in his life – support nieces and nephews, Ficino was well aware that most of his readers had to work. He has practical advice to give on this score, too. First of all he remarks that everyone on earth is suited to some kind of honourable work, whether it is a career or a way of life. The most unfortunate people are those who either waste their talents idly or are forced to do work that is unsuited to their skills. Once again, he begins from the horoscope. Everyone has a ruling planet, and the nature of this planet will determine the guardian angel or daimon who will suggest the right occupation. Rules for this process can be found in most astrology textbooks: Jupiter types might take to law, Venus types to art and so on. Only when one is following the right course will life go smoothly.

What's more, it is essential to live in the right place. The way to determine this is to check one's spirits and physical health; wherever one feels most alert and vigorous is the place to settle. Ficino recommends somewhere within easy reach of the country, for a stay there will refresh the energy that living (let alone working) in a city exhausts. What a modern viewpoint this is, and how relevant the advice! Truly, Ficino stands between the ancient and modern worlds.

A UNIVERSE OF LOVE

By separating out an inner circle of Orphic initiates from an outer circle of people for whom he prescribed different forms of magic, Ficino was following in the footsteps of the ancient mystics such as Pythagoras. He knew that truth must be approached carefully and through a long process of preparation; therefore the deepest secrets are concealed until the initiate is ready for them. Plato reports Socrates on his deathbed observing that although in the Dionysian rites all the celebrants carry the ceremonial wand (thyrsus), the true Bacchae are few. He means that very few taking part truly make contact with the divine forces invoked.

Socrates' remark can sound somewhat dismissive, but that was not Ficino's outlook. His Christian faith gave him the profound conviction that God is pure love, and that he created the universe as an act of love. It is love that holds the universe together, for love unites while discord separates. Love keeps the world working harmoniously, and love leads us back to the Divine. Thus we should love as much as possible, beginning with each other.

Ficino takes as his template Diotima's speech about the Mysteries of love in Plato's *Symposium*. He distinguishes between two kinds of love: that of the body and that of the soul. Physical love works to propagate the species, but spiritual love raises the lover to the Divine. It is from Ficino that we derive the phrase 'Platonic love', for he believed that an unconsummated love refined the soul, whereas sexual expression coarsened it. Like Dante, Ficino loved without possessing and through this love elevated his soul. His beloved was Giovanni Cavalcanti, a well-born Florentine eleven years younger than himself. They remained lifelong friends, although the relationship caused Ficino much heartache in the early years. He called Cavalcanti his 'hero', deriving the word from the Greek word for love, eros.

But for Ficino, love was too precious to be hoarded all for one person. He cultivated many close friendships as well, expressing his affection for his friends in the strongest terms and rating friendship extremely highly. 'Nothing in life is more rarely acquired, or more dearly possessed' he says (*Letters* vol. 2, 63). Often he uses astrological rules for this purpose: synastry, or the comparison of horoscopes. Traditional astrology includes rules for analysing how two people will relate to each other, according to the positions of the planets in their respective horoscopes. Ficino goes somewhat further, and develops the idea that two people influenced by the same planet will enjoy an innate sympathy. Since by Neoplatonic understanding the planets are under the control of divine spirits, this means that one spirit will guide and unite two such people. This spirit is, in fact, the personal daimon or guardian spirit as described by Plotinus.

For example, he writes to Lorenzo di Pierfrancesco de' Medici (a cousin of Lorenzo the Magnificent), telling him that the Sun and the planets Mercury and Venus allot the personal daimon, according to where they are in the horoscope. Since both Ficino and Lorenzo have similar planetary placements, they have 'not just similar spirits, but rather one and the same' (*Letters* vol. 6, 16).

Yet only two days later, Ficino writes to his friend Alberto Lisci in terms that show the two men had somehow fallen out, urging him to remember that since they both have Aquarius rising, Saturn has imparted to them 'just one spirit' that binds them in divine and eternal friendship. It seems that simple need allowed Ficino to claim two quite different guardian spirits within two days. Such a freely creative use of astrological symbolism demonstrates Ficino's flexible attitude to the rules of astrology: in this, as in magic, he was original and innovative.

Ficino lived by his own rule: that to receive, one must first give. 'The one guardian of life is love, but to be loved you must love' (*Letters* vol. 2, 62).

A CULTURE OF MAGIC

Renaissance Florence was in some ways a very modern culture, based as it was on the riches derived from banking and commerce. However, in the fifteenth century science as we know it was not yet in existence, and the world was seen through the lens of the imagination as well as through reason.

Although Ficino devoted himself to private theurgical practices, as someone whose fortunes in life were inextricably linked with the Medici

– effectively the ruling family of Florence – he could hardly hope to live in obscurity. In fact, he was well known and respected as a magician and astrologer. He gave the Medici the benefit of his astrological knowledge on many occasions, for example warning Lorenzo of a difficult planetary transit to his horoscope so that he might be on his guard against danger. That is a more urgent and significant piece of advice than it might appear, since only two years previously to Ficino's warning, the plotters of the Pazzi Conspiracy had murdered Lorenzo's brother Giuliano and almost succeeded in killing Lorenzo himself. Ficino had been on friendly terms with some of the conspirators and needed to reassure Lorenzo that he was on his side.

On a happier occasion, Lorenzo consulted Ficino about refurbishing one of his beautiful estates, Poggio a Caiano. He wanted to make his villa there into an ideal country retreat where philosophical banquets could be held in peaceful surroundings, and he recruited Ficino to choose the correct astrological time for the work to start. Sadly, Lorenzo died before the estate was finished to his satisfaction, but the villa still stands and can be visited. What is more, it seems to have retained to some extent the esoteric purpose for which Lorenzo had intended it. About thirty years after Lorenzo's death, the main salon of the villa was decorated with a profoundly mystical painting, which we shall explore in the next chapter.

Ficino also chose the foundation time for the grand palace built by Filippo Strozzi, a rival of the Medici. This building is in the city of Florence and, like the villa at Poggio, has survived intact until the present day – indeed, it was the Strozzi family seat right up until 1937. Clearly Ficino's astrological skill has long-lasting effects!

Such was Ficino's fame that he even sent advice to the Pope and kings. For example, he wrote a lengthy homily to King Ferdinand Ferrante of Naples, supposedly from his deceased father Alfonso, early in 1479. Ferdinand was then allied with Sixtus IV against Florence, which did not prevent Ficino from describing him as the 'guardian of peace' (Letters vol. 5, 24).

Ficino roughed out a horoscope for Ferdinand, characterizing this forceful enemy as ruled by Mars and Saturn, the two malefics connected with war and hardship. He exhorted Ferdinand to treat with compassion those of his fellows ruled by the same planets. In case Ferdinand did not know that Florence was traditionally considered to be ruled by Mars,

Ficino (having already confessed to being under Saturn himself) specified that his own 'people ... are those ruled by Capricorn or Aquarius, the abodes of Saturn' (*Letters* vol. 5, 28). In other words, he was pleading with Ferdinand to spare Florence, and also – since he had the Sun rising in Capricorn – Lorenzo de' Medici himself. Astrology here subtly serves a political purpose, yet Ficino's concern is also to draw the mind's eye upwards, to turn Ferdinand's soul towards the ascent to God.

THE IMMORTALITY OF THE SOUL

Exorcism was one of Ficino's particular talents, and he writes with justifiable pride of having driven out two troublesome Saturnian spirits (what we would call poltergeists) from an old house, using a ritual involving lights and incense. Such was his reputation that after his death a story went round that his own spirit had appeared to his close friend, the monk Michele Mercati. During life, the two had enjoyed discussing the immortality of the soul and had agreed that whoever died first would return to tell the other about the afterlife. Late one evening Mercati heard a horse's hoofs outside his door. Rushing out, he saw Ficino on a white horse crying, 'Oh Michele, Michele, everything we said is utterly true!' before galloping off into the dark. Michele later learned that Ficino had died that night.

We know that Ficino saw life in the Orphic manner: as a dream. In his work *On the Immortality of the Soul* Ficino writes that divine reality alone is true, and only the philosopher who focuses his attention on the Divine awakens from the dream of life. Those who lust after material things are lost when they die, for they merely replace one set of illusions with another. But the true philosopher – the lover of truth – sees the reality of the highest truth that lies beyond Socrates' 'ocean of beauty'.

During his life, this most mild and melancholy of men strove in all that he did to teach those around him, each on the level suitable to their abilities, just how to turn towards the Divine, while at the same time enjoying to the full the glorious, magical harmony of the world. Even today, we can find in Ficino's books and letters the soundest advice for living in the world; so subtly does Ficino write that meditation on his words reveals increasingly deep secrets. He opens for us, as for his Renaissance friends, the Mysteries of the ancient Greek world.

SECRET
ARTS

SO SECRET WAS FICINO'S Academy that its very existence has become a matter of debate. What is certain is that Ficino, an immensely influential figure in many fields, including religion, politics, magic and art, was at the centre of a group of men who met regularly to celebrate the ancient wisdom of Orpheus, Pythagoras, Plato and Plotinus. And they were bonded by one rather curious trait: they considered themselves to be powerfully influenced by the qualities of the planet Saturn.

> To operate magic is nothing other than to marry the world.
> — Pico della Mirandola, *900 Theses* (9–11)

SATURN AND HIS CHILDREN

In astrology, Saturn is the planet of limits and frustration. Traditionally it was called malefic, or bad; Saturn brings illness and poverty and is especially powerful in old age. Its influence is a depressive one, and it affects other planets adversely too. The person who has Saturn strongly placed in the horoscope is likely to be rather melancholy as a result. Ficino inherited all this traditional belief, which affected him deeply because his own horoscope was strongly marked by Saturn. Indeed, in his life he had plenty of evidence of Saturn's difficult influence. He claimed never to have enjoyed one single day of good health; one illness was so severe that he almost died, but a prayer to the Virgin saved him. He developed cataracts, a severe disability for someone who read and wrote for his living and a cruel one since he so loved the light. He was always short of money. His love for Giovanni Cavalcanti tormented him for years before he was able to come to terms with it. All in all, Saturn, he complained, 'impressed the seal of melancholy on me from the beginning' (*Letters*, vol. 2, p.33).

Faced with such a seemingly negative set of influences, Ficino, believing as he did that 'everything comes from the Good' (*Letters*, vol. 2, p.51), needed by his own rules of harmony to find a positive interpretation. Happily, in his ancient sources he discovered much that was good in Saturn. In Plato's Laws, for instance, he read of Saturn presiding over an Age of Gold. During that early period of mankind, mortals were still in touch with the gods and Saturn was a benign force representing the higher qualities of the mind such as reason.

The scheme of the universe as Ficino and his Neoplatonic sources understood it placed the sphere of Saturn just below the circle of fixed stars and the ultimate Divinity. The spiritual influence raining down from the Divine then passed through the other planets until finally it reached the Earth, at the most grossly material end of the cosmos. Since man is a microcosm of the cosmos, Saturn became associated with the most spiritual part of the human – the mind – and its ability to draw the philosopher from the petty concerns of earthly existence and elevate him to the Divine. We have already seen that Ficino places meditation, the highest step of his sevenfold therapy, under Saturn.

In the *Corpus Hermeticum* Ficino read of the soul's descent from heaven through the planetary spheres, picking up as it went the characteristics of each particular planet. From the Neoplatonist writer Macrobius, he learned of its purifying journey back up through the spheres to the Divine. Ficino began to interpret the pain Saturn caused as a series of tests to refine and cleanse the soul. Suffering under Saturn thus actually became a privilege unknown to more carefree people. It is thanks to Ficino that we still call grim people 'saturnine'. What's more, he connected this purifying yet painful Saturn with the tendency to melancholy exhibited by so many philosophers and poets. Here he drew upon Aristotle, who thought that the habit of deep thought produced physical effects that affected the emotions. Ficino developed this theory in great detail and wrote about it in his book *On Caring for the Health of Learned People*, in which he suggested remedies.

The very nature of study is Saturnian, requiring as it does solitude and serious thought. Thus the Saturnian scholar must make sure he gets enough exercise, nourishing foods and cheerful company. Yet he must retain a strong discipline if he is to succeed in his studies, so a sense of restraint is needed. These guidelines also apply to all who deal in esoteric matters, such as magicians and alchemists. Indeed, for Ficino the practising magician and astrologer, there were no clear boundaries between scholarly pursuits and studies that we today would consider to be arcane.

Ficino's idea of Saturnian gloom and inspiration was to have far-reaching effects. Here is the birth of the outsider artist, the suffering and misunderstood genius, and such was the power of the idea that suddenly everybody wanted to be a Saturnian and to claim his 'unique and divine gift' of singular talent and intelligence, even at the price of a tendency to depression. Within the Academy, itself an exclusive body, there was an elite inner circle known as the Saturnines, among whom Lorenzo the Magnificent was the most illustrious. His horoscope certainly qualified him to be so, since he was born with the Sun rising in Capricorn, making him doubly Saturnian. This inner clique felt special bonds to each other but also to Plato himself, whose supposed horoscope placed Saturn in Libra, a sign of 'elevation' or strength, as well as the Ascendant and three planets in Aquarius, one of the signs that Saturn rules. Thus these men saw themselves as connecting across time with their most revered teacher and sharing in his genius. Ficino promised the philosophers in the Academy that by coming to know their Saturn, they would contemplate arcane celestial secrets. Through his studies Ficino had been able to perfect a psychological initiation that combined the dark descent into suffering of the Eleusinian Mysteries with the revelation of divine light. The deprivation, ill health and mental anguish brought by Saturn became a gateway to loftiest contemplation and – finally – ecstatic union with the Divine.

THE COUNT AND THE KABBALAH

However, there are dangers in such an outlook. Saturn's ambivalent gifts were enough to drive men either into an inflated sense of their genius or into despair. While Ficino himself inclined to introspective melancholy, other geniuses of his time became intoxicated with the sense that a human being has divine potential. Such was Count Pico della Mirandola, Ficino's younger contemporary and close friend of Poliziano. Pico was well qualified as a Saturnian, his horoscope placing Saturn along with Mercury and Venus in the sign of Aquarius, all in aspect to Pico's Moon. Born into an aristocratic family in 1463, he was a precocious genius who wrote the definitive statement of the Renaissance magus in 1486, his *Oration on the Dignity of Man.* This stirring document served as an introduction to his *900 Theses,* in which he believed he had laid the foundation for universal knowledge and which he presented for debate in Rome with any scholars who might be interested. The theses consist of short statements, including gnomic utterances on magic and the Kabbalah, the mystic aspect of Judaism, originally an oral teaching but later written down. Pico even claims that the Kabbalah can 'prove' the divinity of Christ.

Not surprisingly, Church authorities deemed several of these theses heretical, so not only did Pico not have the chance of debating them but he found himself flung into prison. Thanks largely to Lorenzo the Magnificent's intervention, he was eventually released to live under Lorenzo's protection and returned to Florence to live in relative seclusion. The story goes that astrologers accurately predicted his untimely death. Both Pico and his beloved friend Poliziano died mysteriously by arsenic poisoning in 1494, two years after the death of Lorenzo.

Pico is hugely important in the history of arcane knowledge for two reasons. Not only does his *Oration on the Dignity of Man* give a blueprint of the learned magician, but he also introduced the use of Kabbalistic learning into the mix of magic that Ficino had moulded together from ancient sources. Pico's understanding of the magician's role reflects his character. Whereas Ficino saw mankind as occupying a link in the great Chain of Being, between the angels and the animals, Pico gives him absolute freedom. In the Oration he says that when God created the world, he completed it before making man. Hence there was no place for man, no particular gift to bestow upon him. God placed man in the centre of the universe and announced that his nature was unlimited; he could be anything he wanted. He might choose to indulge his senses and degenerate to the life of an animal or even a plant, or he might become a philosopher and become the equal of the angels. Or, best of all, he might meditate and unite with the 'solitary darkness' of God. In this final aim Pico agrees with Ficino and all mystics. But in his turbulent life – which included almost getting killed while abducting another man's wife – he seems not to have practised withdrawing 'into the solitary watch-tower of the mind' (*Letters*, vol. 1, p.51) as Ficino did, but rather acted with a complete disregard for consequences.

Even Pico's description of the ascent to God is framed in rather arrogant terms. He speaks of 'despising' heavenly things, of striving to outdo the angels themselves. Rich, intelligent, healthy and handsome, he had none of Ficino's disadvantages to restrain his confidence. Thus is born the image of the magus whose power knows no bounds – a dangerously intoxicating idea that proved irresistable to later magicians.

THE SIGNIFICANCE OF NUMBERS

Pico studied Hebrew and became interested in Kabbalistic studies early in his career. In 1486 he commissioned Flavius Mithridates to translate from Hebrew a whole Kabbalistic library, comprising most of the known works. Pico and his contemporaries believed the texts they studied were truly ancient, that the authors were figures from the Old Testament such as Abraham. Although in this (as in their belief in the antiquity of the *Corpus Hermeticum*) they were wrong, they were right in that the texts enshrined a form of wisdom handed down at least from the first century BCE.

Study of the Kabbalah revealed to Pico the mystical significance of language, for each Hebrew letter has a numerical significance. Manipulation of the numbers involved can reveal hidden meanings, one word being substituted for another with the same total. Since there are many ways to practise this art (known as gematria), it can be a lifetime's study. Pico considered the Kabbalah to be essential to the successful practice of magic, saying 'No magical operation can be of any efficacy unless it has annexed to it a work of Kabbalah' (Farmer, p.499). However, he was not always consistent. While one of his theses states that only Hebrew names are magically effective, another says that the Orphic hymns are the most powerful magic of all. But magicians henceforth were eager to include Kabbalistic formulae in their repertoire, perhaps partly because the Hebrew alphabet added an alluring mystique.

Pico's untimely and mysterious death also added a romantic gloss to his precocious learning. Times were changing, too. When Lorenzo died, the golden age of Medici patronage of esoteric learning ended with him. The tolerant and open mental attitudes that characterized early Renaissance

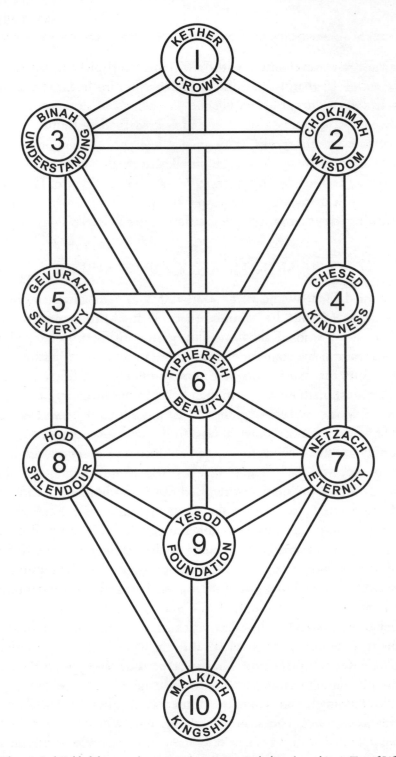

The mystical Kabbalah enters the magician's repertoire, including the sephirotic Tree of Life.

Florence flipped over into a climate of remorseful piety under the sway of the monk Savonarola. Invading French forces marched into the city on the very day of Pico's funeral. His life represents a critical moment when the revival of ancient Mysteries moved from focusing on union with the Divine to gaining power on earth.

THE BLACK DOG

The magicians who followed Ficino and Pico are still famous names: Agrippa, Paracelsus, Giordano Bruno, Tommaso Campanella. None of these men were easy personalities; all seemed to attract trouble. Henry Cornelius Agrippa is typical. Born in Cologne in 1486, he led a restless life moving between France, Germany and Italy. Often accused of heresy, he was so famous in his day that legends grew up around him. One of these claimed that he was accompanied by a familiar spirit in the shape of a black dog, which he let loose as he was dying while fleeing a death sentence for heresy.

Agrippa spent much time writing and revising a monumental three-volume work on magic, *Three Books on Occult Philosophy*, which he completed in 1510 but did not publish until 1533 after many revisions. Not only was the format clearly borrowed from Ficino's *Three Books on Life*, but he also quoted both Ficino and Pico verbatim throughout the work. However, he does not use Ficino's natural magic in quite so innocent a way as it was meant: he harnesses its power to bind the planetary angels to his will. This is treading on very different ground from the philosophical purification that Ficino pursued. Agrippa also makes use of the Kabbalah for similar ends. It is hardly surprising that he gained the reputation of having conjured daimons – but now we are talking about bad daimons, in the Christian sense of demons.

Venturing into such dangerous territory has little to do with the ancient Mysteries and the attempts of Renaissance philosophers to reinvigorate them in contemporary terms. The mystery of Agrippa is that he twice published thorough-going refutations of magic. Indeed, he brought out a book arguing the futility of all human knowledge, including magic, in 1531 and then proceeded to publish *The Occult Philosophy* in 1533 – but appended to this comprehensive handbook of magic the chapters refuting magic from his previous work. Scholars still argue over whether and how deeply Agrippa believed in the magic he both professed and denied. He may have been trying to persuade the Church that he was not really practising magic, or he may have vacillated over its effectiveness. Whatever the case, for our purposes it is enough to know that through Agrippa's work, Ficino's natural magic reached a huge audience, albeit in modified form. *The Occult Philosophy* was the most influential magical work of the Renaissance period.

Its use was not restricted to practising and aspiring magicians. We know that at least one artist, Albrecht Dürer, used it as a source for creating his mysterious engraving Melencholia I. The title seems to refer to Agrippa's classification of the types of melancholy, the first type being the one that afflicts artists. So here we have Ficino's Saturnian sadness pictured for the first time: magic and the hidden knowledge are summed up in a single powerful image. The engraving shows a winged woman sitting idle, a compass in her hand and other instruments scattered around. The very density of the symbolic items and the constricted space of the picture suggest a saturnine atmosphere, yet in the distance a bright star sends out powerful beams against a dark sky. The Divine calls from the heavenly realms: the solitary philosopher may even be meditating upon its presence.

BOTTICELLI'S MYSTERIES

Dürer was just one of many artists who encoded mysteries into their work. Here we must go back a little to Ficino's lifetime, for such was the profound influence of the rediscovered ancient knowledge that it penetrated art and architecture as well as philosophy. Indeed, Lorenzo de' Medici surrounded himself with artists as well as men of learning. The Renaissance is an extraordinary time in art, marking the point when it breaks free from the tyranny of religious subject matter. Portraits now came into vogue, and scenes from ancient Greek myths became popular. Rich men vied with each other to commission artists whose work would lend them a gloss of sophistication. Botticelli and Leonardo da Vinci rubbed shoulders with philosophers in the Medici household, and they produced paintings that required an education in secret knowledge. As one art historian has said, many Renaissance paintings 'were designed for initiates' (Wind, p.15).

Ficino himself may have inspired the design for Botticelli's painting Venus and Mars, now in the National Gallery, London. At this period it was common practice for a painting to be commissioned to a patron's requirements, and often those requirements were elaborated by a man of learning such as Ficino.

Botticelli depicts Venus reclining as she gazes at Mars, who is so deeply asleep after having made love that not even the little satyr blowing a conch shell in his ear can wake him. Other satyrs play with his armour, making fun of his reputation as a war god now that he is helpless and vulnerable. Venus, meanwhile, is unruffled and cool, perfectly poised. The bushes behind her may be myrtle, which is her sacred plant. Clothed in white and chastely dressed, she seems to symbolize spiritual love. Mars, naked and worn out, and mocked by goatish satyrs, would then represent lust. The painting might be a visual representation of one of Ficino's astrological observations from his commentary on Plato's *Symposium*:

> Venus often shackles, so to speak, the malignancy of Mars, by coming into conjunction or opposition with him, or by receiving him or by watching him from the trine or sextile aspect. (Sears, p.97)

It is pretty clear that Venus has already 'received' Mars, but there is a hidden clue that would only be apparent to a viewer who both knew Ficino's quotation and had a smattering of astrological knowledge. The novelist Linda Proud has pointed out that the angle between the two lounging figures is 120 degrees – in astrological terms, a trine aspect. 'Aspect' means 'look' and that is exactly what Venus is doing – looking at Mars from a trine aspect, secure in her superiority. Spiritual love conquers lust, just as Diotima promised in the *Symposium*.

THE MYTHICAL SPRING

One of Botticelli's most famous paintings, the Primavera, may also conceal a meaning derived from the secret wisdom. This painting has never been satisfactorily decoded and multiple interpretations are possible. What does seem clear is that it shows mythical figures who are loosely linked. In the centre is Venus, making a gesture of welcome. Above her head

Botticelli's Primavera still enchants and baffles viewers. It seems to show the journey of the soul into the world and back to the Divine.

is Cupid and to her right (our left) are the Three Graces and Mercury. The three mysterious figures on the right of the painting are a little more obscure: they represent the wind Zephyr and the nymph Chloris whom he pursued and won by violence: he then made amends by transforming her into Flora, the figure of spring who scatters flowers.

What on earth could all this mean? Although there is no documentary proof, it could be that the painting represents the fall of the soul into the material world and its return, through love, to the Divine. On the right-hand side of the painting Chloris may represent the soul, expelled from heaven by the winged Zephyr and lightly clad in her transparent 'astral body'. Arriving on the earth, she enjoys the life of the senses, symbolized by Flora with her flowers. All the movement on this side of the painting is downward and inward, pointing to the material world and simultaneously leading the eye across to Venus. The goddess of love stands at the centre point, for, as we know from Diotima, love can either express itself through the physical world or it can elevate the lover to the realms of spirit. While the right side of the painting shows the former, down-rushing movement, the left side reverses the action. Venus, the Graces and Mercury all reach upward, towards the Divine. The Three Graces are themselves representative of the threefold journey of the soul that comes from the Divine, exists in the world and then returns to God.

Cupid aims his arrow, flaming with divine love, at the central Grace, who indicates her desire by gazing at Mercury – and he turns his back on the scene, perfectly detached and focused on stirring some little clouds with his staff or caduceus. Mercury, the god of knowledge and the leader of souls to the Underworld, is the keeper and interpreter of secrets. We remember at this point that the mythical sage Hermes Trismegistus takes his name. Later, we shall see Mercury's central role in revealing the mysteries of alchemy. Here, he is the guide back to the world of spirit and the Divine. In other words, this painting may show the entire Mystery of the soul's fate according to the ancient wisdom.

The painting seems to have been commissioned by Lorenzo de' Medici's brother Giuliano, but when he was tragically murdered in 1478, the painting was altered slightly and passed to Lorenzo di Pierfrancesco de' Medici, a cousin of Lorenzo. Ficino wrote a long letter to this young man that has been linked to the Primavera. In it, he describes an ideal horoscope in which Venus symbolizes human nature. But Ficino's view is that we only become fully human when we fulfil our divine potential. He warns Lorenzo di Pierfrancesco:

> Beware that you never despise it, perhaps thinking that human nature is born of earth, for human nature herself is a nymph ... She was born of an heavenly origin and was beloved above others by an ethereal god. For indeed, her soul and spirit are love and kinship; her eyes are majesty and magnanimity; her hands are liberality and greatness in action; her feet, gentleness and restraint. Finally, her whole is harmony and integrity, honour and radiance.
>
> (*Letters*, vol. 4 pp.62–3)

Ficino's second sentence could refer to the nymph Chloris and her lover Zephyr as well as suggesting the figure of Venus herself. No wonder the painting has such a mysterious and compelling atmosphere. Its celebrated beauty has an enigmatic quality because it may just be portraying the central mystery of human existence: our spiritual origins and destiny. And that story is as relevant today as it was to Ficino and his friends.

A RECLUSIVE ARTIST

The Primavera depicts an idealized rural setting with fruit trees and flower-sprinkled grass, and Lorenzo de' Medici sought to create such a setting in reality at Poggio a Caiano. We have already seen that Ficino chose the time for some important building work there. The whole place is steeped in the ancient wisdom, for it is here that Lorenzo presided over meetings of his closest friends, perhaps the elusive Academy itself. The building is designed in imitation of the rural retreats so beloved by rich Romans, so it is classical in style with a dramatic pillared entrance or portico imitating a temple. A terracotta frieze representing classical figures of myth and allegory tops the portico. It is possible to see the frieze as an illustration of Neoplatonic doctrines, for example of the journey of the soul. The visitor who had some knowledge of the ancient doctrines would feel that he was truly entering a temple where arcane secrets would be discussed.

When Lorenzo died, sadly young, in 1492, the villa passed to his son Giovanni, who later became Pope Leo X. Giovanni had spent his youth among Lorenzo's close friends, including Ficino and Pico, so he had been well educated in Neoplatonic and magical ideas – something that was not unusual in church dignitaries at that time. He began an ambitious programme of decoration in the villa honouring the most famous members of his family, including Lorenzo. One of the artists involved, Jacopo da Pontormo, was commissioned to paint a lunette high on one end wall of the main salon or reception room. This painting has, like the Primavera, retained its mystery despite many attempts at interpretation.

Pontormo was a peculiarly apt choice for this villa of mysteries. Born in 1494, he typified the withdrawn and moody genius that Dürer represents in Melencholia I. Unlike most artists of that time, who juggled as many commissions as possible with the help of a large workshop of apprentices, Pontormo preferred to work with a single helper. Such was his need for privacy and secrecy that when he worked on site he usually erected barriers around himself and his painting. He shared his house with whoever was his apprentice at any particular time, but was notorious for withdrawing into an upper room accessible only by ladder and ignoring visitors. When he worked, he would sometimes spend whole days simply standing and gazing at the unfinished painting. As he aged he became increasingly reclusive, spending more and more time at home drawing.

We know an unusual amount about Pontormo because for the last three years of his life he kept a diary, detailing his health, diet and working arrangements. Evidence strongly suggests that he understood at least the basic principles of astrology and was trying to keep himself in good health during a difficult period of Saturnine influence – and that he was using the advice given in Ficino's Three Books on Life to do so. Both Pontormo's diet and his daily habits closely conform to Ficino's directions for scholars and for ageing people. Pontormo was known for his intelligence and learning – so much so that Vasari, the Renaissance biographer of artists, complained that his paintings were difficult to understand. Clearly Pontormo considered himself to be one of the people to whom Ficino was addressing his advice; indeed, he had the evidence of his horoscope and personality to prove that he was one of Saturn's children.

Pontormo's habits of solitude, withdrawal and apparent inactivity may well reflect his absorption of Ficino's descriptions of Saturnian contemplation in his third book of life, *On Obtaining Life from the Heavens*. This is the most magical of the three books, full of instructions for using astrology to time crucial events and for making talismans. Pontormo in his attic room, ignoring callers, may have been practising the seventh and highest step of Ficino's planetary 'ladder' of instructions for good physical and spiritual health. Although we cannot prove this, Pontormo's paintings offer eloquent evidence of his intense inner spiritual life. No other painter of the period produced such otherworldly images that, like Ficino's image of the universe, can themselves induce a meditative state in the thoughtful viewer.

So we see that Ficino's 'exoteric' advice reached far and wide, pene-trating the artistic community both during his life and after his death. But did Pontormo know the more esoteric teachings such as the Orphic Hymns? Although he cannot have heard them from Ficino, he may well have been aware of the existence of the ancient Mystery cults. Pontormo understood astrology and had many learned friends. The fresco he painted for the salon at Poggio a Caiano suggests that he understood the esoteric aspects of the villa where Lorenzo had celebrated Platonic Mysteries with his friends.

ELEUSIS IN A MEDICI VILLA

The decoration of the salon, although it took many years to complete, is designed as a whole. Round the walls are historical scenes referring to the triumphs of Cosimo and Lorenzo de' Medici. At either end, higher up, are two frescos showing not history but myths. The orientation of the villa is important. Pontormo's fresco is at the southeast end, while at the other is a fresco by Alessandro Allori (the apprentice of Pontormo's favourite pupil Bronzino) of the Garden of the Hesperides. In Neoplatonic lore, these positions correspond to Capricorn and Cancer, traditionally known as the gates through which souls enter the world (Cancer) and leave it (Capricorn). The frieze over the villa's portico probably refers to this myth as well.

Pontormo's fresco, known as Vertumnus and Pomona, has been compared to Botticelli's Primavera, and with good reason. Like the Primavera, it has never been conclusively interpreted – yet both paintings appear to refer to the Mysteries. In Pontormo's fresco, eight figures are seated on two levels of a wall while two more sit in foliage above them. The woman at the far right holds a pruning hook as if on guard, keeping the viewer at bay. The wall seems to be a barrier beyond which is some kind of sacred ground. We can guess at this because three figures have items associated with the Eleusinian Mysteries. Both the old man on the far left and the younger man next to him hold baskets, which could represent the kistai, or sacred baskets, that figured largely in the Mysteries. The girl with her back to the viewer seems to be concealing something that could be a *kernos*, or tray, on which mystical items were displayed.

The four figures on the lower level of the wall appear to be the celebrants, while on the upper level we see two of the gods of the Mysteries. Demeter can be recognized by the corn and poppies in her headdress, while Dionysus appears naked. Nudity in Renaissance art often signifies 'naked truth' and here it hints at direct revelation such as the celebrants experienced at Eleusis.

In this villa where Ficino and Lorenzo sang Orphic hymns and celebrated the Mysteries, the latter's son created a memorial to that time. But it is more than that: it is a meditation on the most ancient Mysteries that, like the Primavera, still speaks to us today. It is a painting created for initiates, and it takes time and meditation to penetrate its meaning. There are many more paintings like this in churches and villas in Italy and art galleries throughout the world that reveal secret wisdom to anyone who is patient enough to spend time with them.

MAGICAL BUILDINGS

We have seen how a building such as Poggio could enshrine esoteric lore in its very fabric, as well as being built at an astrologically significant time. Poggio was not an isolated case. Ficino's ideas about harmony vibrating throughout the whole universe could be applied to architecture as well as music and art, but even earlier than Ficino, his fellow-Florentine Filippo Brunelleschi had designed buildings using proportions that not only made them harmonious but also imbued them with mystical meaning. Brunelleschi based his designs on classical buildings, a decision in itself indicative of his appreciation of the ancient wisdom. In one of his most celebrated buildings, the Ospedale degli Innocenti, he used the proportions one to two, one to five and two to five. These proportions create a serene harmony that the viewer can appreciate without understanding how it is created. But Brunelleschi almost certainly used these proportions for symbolic reasons: for example, Christ suffers five wounds and five is the esoteric number of mankind.

Brunelleschi's buildings still exert a strange fascination, as anyone who has visited the Old Sacristy in San Lorenzo or the Pazzi Chapel will know. Both these buildings are decorated inside with astrological frescoes. These perfectly proportioned, jewel-like buildings are studded throughout Florence as mystical reminders of a knowledge that has now faded from our pursuit of the arts.

The other great architect of the Renaissance, Leon Battista Alberti, defined beauty as 'the harmony and concord of all the parts, achieved in such a manner that nothing could be added, taken away or altered' (Hartt, p.223). Alberti was another of the true Renaissance men, skilled in literature, astrology, cryptography and architecture. His buildings express his belief in the essential value of harmony to a high degree, achieved by the careful use of number and proportion. In his unfinished Malatesta Temple in Rimini, the sense of cosmic harmony created by the design of the building is complemented in the interior by low relief carvings of the planets. As in Brunelleschi's sacred buildings, ancient Pagan wisdom rubs shoulders quite happily with Christian symbols. That harmonious co-existence was one of the great achievements of the Renaissance. The ancient wisdom was not rejected as heretical but valued as a timeless knowledge that belonged to no one culture or religion but to anyone who had the determination to discover and apply it to their lives.

SPEAKING WITH ANGELS

THE HEADY PROMISES of magical power that infused Renaissance culture in Italy were too enticing to be confined to that country. Ficino corresponded with like-minded men across Europe and books of magic found a huge and eager audience as the invention of printing made them more accessible. A case in point is John Dee (1527–1608), the English magus who lived during the reigns of Elizabeth I and James I. The atmosphere of Elizabeth's court was suffused with myth and magic, as she inspired a brilliant circle of poets and talented men who vied with each other to mythologize her as the Faery Queen, presiding over a Golden Age.

> The entire universe is like a lyre tuned by
> some excellent artificer …
>
> — John Dee,
> *An Aphoristic Introduction*, xi

QUEEN ELIZABETH'S MAGICIAN

During Elizabeth's reign, poetry and paintings were infused with rich symbolism hinting at mysteries. The English Renaissance came into flower and cultured men immersed themselves in the writings of Ficino and the ancient philosophers whose wisdom he had unearthed and interpreted anew. Dee stands at the heart of this explosion of knowledge. He accumulated an extraordinary library of four thousand books and manuscripts, among which could be found all Ficino's and Pico della Mirandola's major works as well as the *Corpus Hermeticum*, Agrippa's

Three Books on Occult Philosophy, works by Dionysius the Areopagite and books on Renaissance architecture. Dee's library was so remarkable that it attracted a constant stream of visitors. Although four thousand books might not seem a great number to us, we should remember that in Dee's day books were comparatively rare and expensive, and manuscripts precious. Even the library at Cambridge University contained only about four hundred works at the time.

So Dee was a man of extraordinary learning. His interests ranged over far wider topics than magic and astrology: he influenced the art of navigation, helped to introduce the study of mathematics (regarded with suspicion in Britain as being semi-magical itself) and mooted the idea of a British Library. He was also one of the first antiquarians, helping to pioneer interest in the physical remains of British history. But all this knowledge reflected his basic fascination with the use of astrology, magic and alchemy for the dual purpose of understanding the physical world and uncovering his own divine nature.

Born in 1527, Dee was the son of a minor official at Henry VIII's court and he inherited the family home at Mortlake, where he amassed his library. He studied at Cambridge, and it was at this point in his life that his esoteric interests began to get him into trouble. In 1546 he used his knowledge of mathematics to make a flying machine for a performance of Aristophanes' comedy *Peace*. The result was awe-inspiring: a giant beetle flew up to the roof of Trinity College hall, carrying on its back a man with a basket of food. Such a spectacle aroused both wonder and fear in the audience, and from that moment on Dee was viewed with a measure of suspicion. He was out of place in Protestant England; in Italy, he would have been revered as much as Ficino or Pico.

So it is no surprise that Dee shortly left for Europe to study and teach. He was a prodigy: at the tender age of 23 he was drawing vast audiences in Paris to his lectures on Euclid. On his return to England, he became tutor to Robert Dudley, later the Earl of Leicester. During the brief reign of Mary Tudor, Dee was asked to draw up her horoscope. He did so, later performing the same task for her half-sister and rival, Elizabeth. Shortly afterwards, he was accused of treason and of trying to enchant the queen, the penalty for which was death. Somehow Dee managed to prove his innocence, but suspicions of dark magical practices were to dog him for the rest of his life. Thankfully, Dee secured the protection of the

IOHANNES DEE,

Londinensis,

*Mathematicus Anglorum Celeberrimus
et Socius Collegii Trin. Cambricensis.
Nat. A. 1527. d. 13. Iulii. Den. A. 1608.
Ex collectione Friderici Roth - Scholtzii.*

John Dee's encyclopaedic learning and proficiency in the occult arts made him an indispensable advisor to Queen Elizabeth I.

Earl of Leicester, who ensured his influence with Elizabeth. Indeed, Dee used astrology to choose the date for her coronation – and Elizabeth's triumphant reign seems to suggest that he chose well. The Queen occasionally favoured him with visits to Mortlake, during which Dee explained to her his mystical philosophy. Yet although she was clearly friendly towards him, his dubious reputation seems to have precluded the possibility of royal patronage in the form of honours and high office.

Dee did not settle quietly under Elizabeth's protection; he travelled on the Continent from time to time and it has been suggested that he spied for Elizabeth – using the code name 007! All this time he was writing and publishing works that reflected the broad range of his expertise. For Dee, the study of mathematics and science was closely allied with magic and astrology. As time passed, he seems to have moved deeper and deeper into what we would now see as a purely magical world, culminating in the years he spent in Europe working with Edward Kelley on summoning angels.

When Dee and Kelley parted company and Dee returned to England in 1589, he found his house in Mortlake broken into and his library ransacked. He had no position and no security until seven long years later when Queen Elizabeth made him Warden of Christ's College, Manchester. However, by now his reputation had turned many against him, and eventually he was forced to give up his post. When James I ascended the throne in 1603, Dee's position worsened. His days of royal protection were now over and since James was notoriously afraid of all things magical, the likelihood of persecution increased. Dee retired to Mortlake with his daughter Katherine, there to live in such poverty that he was often forced to sell books to buy food. This was a sadly ignoble ending for one of Britain's great geniuses. John Dee died in 1608 and his grave remains obscure.

THE LONDON SEAL OF HERMES

Dee's troubled life and impoverished last years serve as an example of how difficult the life of a philosopher-magus can be. We might cast our minds back to Socrates, accused of corrupting youth and receiving the death sentence; to Pythagoras being driven from Croton; to Ficino invoking Lorenzo's support to keep the Church from persecuting him for his magical works. Yet Dee was immensely influential and still is to this day, as we shall see. His early theatrical magic will lead us into the world of Shakespeare and hidden knowledge upon the stage; his summoning of angels shaped the course of ritual magic from the nineteenth century onwards.

Dee's magical philosophy was firmly founded upon the workings of astrology, which he sought to ground in mathematical principles. In this

Elizabeth I, the faery queen

he inherits the mantle of Pythagoras; for both men, number represented an eternal truth that, applied to nature, could give reliable information. In 1558 Dee published his first full-length work, known as *An Aphoristic Introduction*. This consisted of a list of 120 aphorisms on astrology: how it works, what it consists of and how it could be improved (chiefly by refining astronomical observations).

According to Dee, everything that moves emits rays spherically around it, much like a stone causing ripples in a pond. The planets and fixed stars give out both luminous rays and invisible ones, and like seals they imprint their influence on suitable matter. Thus the rays of all celestial bodies are constantly bombarding us, but their influence depends on their strength and on our receptivity. The magician can affect this influence by using the right materials: 'More wonderful things can be performed truly and naturally, without... injury to the Christian religion, than any mortal might be able to believe' (Shumaker, p.125). Here Dee is precisely following Ficino's understanding of natural magic. His 120 aphorisms may also represent a respectful nod towards Pico's 900 Theses. In other words, he is following the trail blazed by the great Italian Renaissance magi.

The world, Dee says, is like a lyre, and man is a microcosm of that harmonious instrument. The magician can play upon the lyre by plucking certain strings and thereby affect not only nature but man too. Here Dee is using an analogy. Unlike Ficino, he himself does not appear to have practised music – but all the same, he is another Orpheus among magi.

What exactly did the Introduction introduce? The clue lies on the title page, which is graced with an elaborate design centred around a mystical symbol that looks rather like a stick man. This is Dee's London Seal of Hermes, or Hieroglyphic Monad, his ultimate answer to all questions. He was in no hurry to write about it, though, and spent the next six years mulling over the great secret he was to put before the public. Then he wrote the *Monas Hieroglyphica* in thirteen days.

The only clear thing about this short work of 24 'theorems' accompanied by diagrams is the symbol itself. It consists of an arrangement of the shapes from which the glyphs of the planets are made; thus, by turning the symbol around, all the planets can be seen in it. Obviously it is an all-inclusive, unifying symbol and it seems that Dee thought that a proper understanding of it could unlock universal knowledge. Elizabeth I was sufficiently impressed by it to visit Dee for instruction on its use. But alas, we are not able to drop into Mortlake to be likewise enlightened.

On one level, the Monas seems to be about alchemy; Dee quotes Hermes Trismegistus and refers to the right astrological time to begin the alchemical process. But on a deeper level he appears to be describing an inner alchemy – the refining of the soul until it is able to return to the Divine while the magus is still in the body. Steeped as he was in the wisdom of Ficino, Pico and the ancient philosophers, Dee felt that he had been able to rediscover their actual experience of the ascent to Divinity. The Monas is his attempt to pass on that knowledge to others. Throughout, he drops hints that those who already have some mystical knowledge will easily understand the work. Others are advised 'whoever does not understand should either learn or be silent' (Suster, p.36). As always, the mystical knowledge is hidden from profane view.

Dee fails to explain in detail how exactly the reader is to learn. However, faced with the London Seal we might cast our minds back to Ficino and his instructions for making an image of the universe on which to meditate. In fact, that is exactly what Dee has done with his symbol. In 1592 Dee wrote to the Archbishop of Canterbury describing his habit of 'ascending ... from things visible to consider of things invisible ... by the most marvellous frame of the whole world, philosophically viewed' (Yates, p.14). Dee, then, is following Ficino's advice exactly, meditating on the symbol as much as possible, applying to it his intuition and imagination (which Dee, like Ficino, valued highly in magical matters). The magus would then meta-morphosize, that is, realize his own divine nature. Since Dee thought he had rediscovered the method of ascent to the Divine, we may suppose that he had succeeded in achieving it himself. Yet he continued his magical quest, entering upon a rather a different type of experience.

DEE'S ANGELIC VISITORS

Dee's conversations with angels have become so notorious as to all but eclipse his other achievements; indeed, they have been the basis for his enduring reputation as a magician of the most dubious kind. While contemporary magicians find inspiration in Dee's angelic magic, academics question how such a polymath and genius could prove so gullible. For Dee himself never saw or heard the angels who communicated with him for years – he always had to use a medium. The most notorious of these was Edward Kelley, who turned up on Dee's doorstep in 1582. Kelley presented himself as 'Edward Talbot' and his history included being expelled from Oxford and being pilloried for forgery. Nevertheless, he either was a skilled medium or he persuaded Dee that he was. The two men worked in partnership for the next seven years, mostly during travels on the Continent during which they had mixed success in finding the patronage they sought.

The method for summoning angels and conversing with them is very different from the mystical ascent through meditation implied in Dee's Monas or the Ficinian astral magic of the Aphorisms. It is ritual magic, involving physical purification and serious piety. Kelley made his first angelic contact by using a crystal ball (now in the British Museum). A being calling itself the angel Uriel responded and gave elaborate instructions for making a table and wax seals engraved with various mystical figures and words. Once this was set up, Uriel began to dictate various magic squares filled with numbers and strange letters from an unknown alphabet. This, Kelley told Dee, was the language of the angels, which later came to be known as Enochian. Other angels began to appear and dictated messages in Enochian, giving each letter by its position in table, column and square, which Dee then had to find. The system is a kind of Kabbalah, although very unlike Pico's version.

Dee and Kelley spent hours at a time at this grindingly slow and laborious business, enlivened from time to time by dramatic visions and visits from beguiling angelic entities such as the young girl Madimi. At first appearing as a rather shy creature, she later manifested to Kelley wantonly naked and ordering the two men to swap wives. Dee was profoundly shocked at being asked to go 'expressly against the commandment of God' (Suster, p.86) and it remains unclear whether or not he complied.

Dee kept meticulous records of angelic sessions that make amazing yet rather wearisome reading. He and Kelley devoted huge amounts of time and energy to receiving mystical knowledge and Dee obviously had complete faith that he truly was learning secrets from a higher source. Yet it is difficult to say exactly what secrets emerged from the sessions. In May

1588 Dee noted in his diary that Kelley 'did open the great secret to me, God be thanked' (Suster, p.93). Does that mean that angels communicated a supreme wisdom through Kelley? Dee is too secretive to say.

Neither Dee nor Kelley flourished after they parted in 1589. Kelley enjoyed some success in Prague as an alchemist but fell from royal favour and died in 1595. Dee returned home to find, as we have seen, his home burgled and his library ransacked. Whatever the 'great secret' was, it did little to sweeten his last years. Yet his angelic diaries lived on to exert a profound influence on later magicians such as Aleister Crowley. Dee remains an enigma and can perhaps stand as an example of the way in which at this period the ancient secret wisdom began to slide into obscurity, covered by complex layers of magical ritual and alchemy.

ANGELS IN PRISON

Although Dee's attempts to reach the hidden wisdom remain problematic, he certainly influenced his contemporaries deeply enough to lead them along the same track that he followed. One of the more notorious of these is Tommaso Campanella (1568–1639), a Neapolitan monk who led an extraordinary life which included 27 years spent in prison for various charges of heresy and fomenting revolution. Campanella believed firmly that a new order of peace and a universal religion was about to begin and that his work – including magic and astrology – was to further it.

Naturally such views did not go down well with the Church, but imprisoning Campanella did not keep him quiet. He wrote to Galileo of being 'buried', yet he wrote busily and – amazingly – got his books into circulation. He also set up horoscopes for his fellow prisoners, and that led to him realizing that one of them had the ability to communicate with spiritual beings. His situation was infinitely harder than that of Dee and Kelley – and yet, somehow Campanella managed to achieve a similar dialogue with mysterious entities. His method involved nothing so complex as the Enochian language; he simply put his fellow-prisoner into a trance and conducted a seance.

Whereas Dee seems always to have trusted his angels, Campanella was more circumspect. They began by giving impressive answers and making prophecies which later came true; however, over time they began to make rather dubious assertions such as that Hell does not exist and that souls reincarnate – neither of which doctrines is acceptable to a Catholic. Campanella finally came to believe that he had contacted both 'devils of evil will, as also good angels' (Walker, p.229).

Astonishingly, some of Campanella's books won him powerful supporters. Eventually he left prison behind him in 1629 and, thanks to some flattering verses he had written to Pope Urban VIII, enjoyed a period of papal protection. He even practised astrological magic in Ficino's style in order to save the Pope from an eclipse that portended his death. Campanella and the Pope carried out a rather delightful ritual in a sealed room within the Vatican, burning aromatic substances associated with the benefic planets Venus and Jupiter in a room decorated with white silk and green branches to attract light and pleasant planetary rays. All that Ficino recommended was done: gentle music was playing and there were precious stones to be worn or held and even astrologically distilled spirits to drink! Candles represented the Sun and Moon and five torches the planets. This aesthetically pleasing ritual seemed to work, since the Pope survived.

Sadly Campanella was not so lucky when, foreseeing his own demise, he tried a similar ritual for himself in 1639: this time, death was not to be cheated. During his life this astonishing man had not only influenced a pope but also championed the new and controversial theories of Copernicus and Galileo. Whatever he achieved was done from a magical perspective, a belief that man's true nature is spiritual. Like Pythagoras, he sought to bring into being a perfect society based on secret wisdom. His fearless spiritual experiments took the secret wisdom a step further into the future.

DEE TREADS THE BOARDS

Campanella shows us how far the influence of Ficino and Dee spread among practising magicians, but the secret wisdom flowed into other channels as well and thrived. Nowhere can this be seen better than in the theatre. At this point we may call to mind the ancient origins of theatre in Greece: all drama was dedicated to Dionysus as a ritual of cleansing and catharsis. Right from its beginnings, theatre has had a strong magical form and purpose, so it is hardly surprising that Dee infiltrates that area of the culture. He was in the right place and time to do so, for London was unique in that respect; it was where James Burbage built the first public theatre in 1576, before which plays had been performed either in the homes of the rich or the courtyards of inns. His success encouraged the building of many more theatres, capable of holding audiences of thousands. No other city in Europe had anything approaching this plethora of venues for drama.

Dee's *Preface to Euclid* included quotes from the classical architect Vitruvius and his great admirer Alberti, both of whom believed that architecture was the supreme art that all other arts and technical knowledge merely existed to enhance. It is highly probable that Dee's enthusiasm influenced Burbage, who was himself a carpenter as well as an actor. The style of his theatre drew on classical sources in an age when building was still medieval in style: nothing like it had ever been seen before. The theatre was an Elizabethan version of a Dionysian ritual arena.

We have already seen Dee's talent for providing spectacular mechanical effects. Now, with public theatres springing up, such effects were in great demand. Magic and the theatre were in close collusion from the beginning. But Dee's influence stretched further than the physical form of the theatre and its machinery: he inspired the content of plays as well. It is thought that Ben Jonson's *The Alchemist* (1610) satirizes Dee in the character of Subtle, a charlatan who offers to work marvels for a series of variously gullible victims. At one point Subtle actually mentions 'one whose name is Dee' (Suster, p.136).

Jonson's plays mock human weakness and ignorance; however, Shakespeare, his contemporary, looked deeper into human nature. In one of his most magical plays, *The Tempest*, he portrays a Renaissance magus in the figure of Prospero. This enigmatic character who orchestrates the entire plot with his magical arts may well be a flattering depiction of Dee. Since *The Tempest* was Shakespeare's last play, it is possible that he chose to end his career with graceful thanks to Dee for his influence on the theatre, showing him as a magus devoted entirely to using magic for good purposes. Prospero's most famous speech even echoes Dee's letter to the Archbishop of Canterbury. Dee had written of 'things transitory and momentary' and of contemplating 'the whole world'. Shakespeare makes Prospero reflect on the insubstantial nature of what we think of as reality:

The cloud-capp'd towers, the gorgeous palaces,
The solemn temples, the great globe itself,
Yea, all which it inherit, shall dissolve …
We are such stuff
As dreams are made on, and our little life
Is rounded with a sleep.

—*The Tempest*, IV, I, ll.152–8

Here is Shakespeare outlining the basic understanding of the ancient philosophers, who saw that they must focus their spiritual energies on eternal truths in order to liberate themselves from the unsatisfying transient world. This speech, given by an idealized Renaissance magus, suggests that there is more to *The Tempest* than mere crowd-pleasing entertainment.

ISLAND OF THE MYSTERIES

Ben Jonson memorably dubbed Shakespeare 'the swan of Avon', thus linking him (perhaps unconsciously) to Orpheus, whom Plato imagined reincarnating as a swan. Shakespeare himself was very aware of the magical powers of music and refers to it often in his plays. He mentions Orpheus by name four times in his works; his own poetic gift certainly places him in the Orphic line of succession. However, any reasonably well-educated man of the Elizabethan age could recount ancient Greek myths from the popular retellings of Ovid. Did Shakespeare have deeper knowledge? There are many hints in his plays that he did. For instance, the climax of *The Winter's Tale* has a supposed statue of the wrongly maligned lady Hermione coming to life. This apparently magical act reflects a notorious passage in the *Corpus Hermeticum* in which Hermes Trismegistus describes the ancient Egyptian priests bringing statues to life by magic.

In *Love's Labours Lost* three lords swear to stay away from women while they devote themselves to study. Of course their resolve is undermined, but the play ends with their intended ladies insisting on them remaining celibate for a year and a day. The main theme of this unusual play is Platonic love and the value of elevating and refining love through contemplation. Therefore it is not by coincidence that one of the suitors is named Berowne – considered by many scholars to be a punning reference to Giordano Bruno, a maverick Italian monk who worked within the Hermetic tradition and was in demand for his esoteric knowledge of alchemy. Bruno visited England in 1582–5, causing a sensation in educated circles and even as far as Elizabeth's court.

Nor is it a coincidence that the theatre in which Shakespeare held shares was called the Globe. The canopy over the stage in this open-air theatre was known as 'the heavens' and was painted with a zodiac. The audience finds itself actually inhabiting an image of the universe as recommended by both Ficino and Dee – a fit place for plays of symbolic and mythical meaning to be staged.

In fact, in *The Tempest* we encounter an entire play that seems to re-enact the original Eleusinian Mysteries. The fantastical plot defied analysis and baffled many commentators until a critic called Colin Still realized the nature of Shakespeare's intention. Still's inspiration was that Shakespeare, himself an initiate into ancient wisdom, had restaged the Mysteries and shown both levels of initiation on stage. Why should he do that? In this, his last play, he seems to have been reaching right back to the original purpose of drama, the celebration of the rites of Dionysus. Drama in Greek times aimed to purify the audience by engaging their most extreme emotions, leaving them at the end of the play cleansed and emptied. Shakespeare's play allows the audience to experience initiation and the final vision of beauty and bliss, along with the characters involved.

THE ELEUSINIAN THREAD

The Tempest recounts the story of Prospero, whose brother Antonio has usurped his Dukedom of Milan (while Prospero was 'rapt in secret studies'). Antonio has Prospero and his daughter Miranda (an echo of Mirandola?) stranded on an island. Happily, Prospero has taken an extensive library with him and settles down to magical studies, turning the island into a realm of enchantment. When Antonio sails by the island with a large retinue, Prospero raises a storm and shipwrecks them. During the course of the play he magically directs their experiences so that wrongdoers are punished and repent and the good are tested and rewarded.

The first hint that we are watching the Mysteries comes with the storm. All the court party undergo a ritual purification in water before they are washed ashore, where they fall asleep. This is a minor experience of death, from which the party awake to find themselves symbolically renewed – their clothes, soaked and stained by the shipwreck, are dry and fresher than before. We may remember that initiates at Eleusis first bathe ritually in the sea and then, before the final rites, dress in clean clothes.

Ferdinand, the son of Alonzo, King of Naples (who helped Antonio depose Prospero), is separated from the main party and follows the sweet music played by the spirit Ariel, who serves Prospero. The music seems to Ferdinand to be for 'some god'; he has already been through the darkness and confusion of the shipwreck and is now on the brink of the Greater Initiation of Eleusis. Then Prospero brings him together with Miranda, a moment that represents the climactic vision of the maiden Persephone.

Yet before Ferdinand can be united with Miranda he must undergo a series of labours as Prospero's servant. In other words, he suffers in a similar way to the suitors in *Love's Labours Lost*. The tale of love being proved by labour is an ancient one, retold from an ancient source by Apuleius in the second century CE as the story of Cupid and Psyche. In Apuleius' tale the beautiful Psyche (which means soul) is loved by Cupid on the understanding that she is not allowed to know who her lover is. Tempted by her sisters into curiosity, she finds out and is banished from his company and forced by Venus to undergo a series of all but impossible tasks before she can win Cupid again.

Ferdinand's trials are similarly a test of the purity of his soul, the implication being that Miranda too is divine – which, as Persephone, she is. Shakespeare hints at this identification by including in the play a masque performed by spirits to celebrate Ferdinand's successful completion of his trials and winning of Miranda's love. Since love is in the air, we might expect the cast to include Venus, but no – the star of the show is Demeter (here called by her Roman name, Ceres). In one speech she makes explicit reference to Persephone's abduction by Pluto and her own subsequent search. As if to underline that this curious interlude is the heart of the play, Shakespeare concludes it with Prospero's speech on the illusory nature of life, as quoted earlier. He then invites Ferdinand into his 'cell' – a magical inner sanctum perhaps referring to the sanctum at Eleusis that only the higher initiates entered. Ferdinand has achieved full initiation.

Meanwhile the other members of the shipwrecked party imagine Ferdinand to be drowned. They plot and bicker their way across the island, meandering and hopelessly lost, sometimes misled by Caliban the trickster spirit. They undergo much the same sort of endurance test that the initiates did at Eleusis, being frightened by darkness and loud noises, sudden lights and the terror of the unknown. But Prospero is playing the hierophant's part, inexorably drawing them towards himself all the time. Finally they come to his hermitage. Here Prospero forgives the wrongdoers Alonzo and Antonio and reveals in his modest dwelling a vision of Ferdinand and Miranda. This ideal 'mystical marriage' is the climax and reward of the Lesser Initiation.

In this, his last play, Shakespeare proves that theatre can still fulfil its original purpose and present the true Mysteries to a receptive audience. As in the Eleusinian Mysteries, the aim is not so much to impart knowledge as to create a profound shared experience that will settle in the soul and work on a deep, unconscious level. The shipwrecked party have been through death and suffering and achieved bliss, and the audience too have witnessed something very like the original Eleusinian Mysteries – in a theatre in south London, during the reign of Elizabeth I.

ORPHEUS REBORN

Shakespeare was articulating a widespread notion of the magical effects of theatrical performance that included dance and song as well as acting. We are looking at an age during which every important occasion would be graced with festivities, whether a simple country dance or an elaborate court masque. The educated court circle was thoroughly versed in ideas of the harmony of the world, which dance and music could so effectively evoke and demonstrate. Wherever Elizabeth I went, she was treated to beautifully staged (and sometimes financially ruinous) theatrical and musical performances by her hosts, for whom it was vital to express their loyalty and respect. These entertainments often depicted Elizabeth herself triumphing in a magical battle against evil forces, restoring the harmony of a world disrupted by black magic.

Ben Jonson developed a remarkable talent for producing masques for his sovereign James I. Although James feared and loathed magic, he was far from averse to being seen as a supernatural power giving life to and protecting his realm. Jonson, who, despite his cruel jibes at Dee, was well read in Ficino and Neoplatonic ideas, used his masques as magical talismans to draw down the influences they represented. He regarded the king as having a particular, sacred power, and in his presence the masques were touched with magic. So, for instance, the Christmas masque The Vision of Delight showed a verdant spring landscape and one of the characters directed attention to the King 'whose presence maketh this perpetual spring' (Greene, p.655). We might even make comparisons with Botticelli's springtime painting Primavera, a similarly talismanic work. Each is intended to direct beneficent forces to its audience or viewer.

The court masques, including as they do both music and dance, are an early form of opera. The first true opera was performed in Italy in 1597 and only a decade later was developed into an art form of genius – by an alchemist. Claudio Monteverdi (1567–1643) is one of the most celebrated of Baroque composers, but few of his musical fans are aware that at his death he merited a sonnet describing him as a 'great master of alchemy'. The practice absorbed him all his life and he wrote that his music expressed Neoplatonic truths. Thus it hardly comes as a surprise to find that Monteverdi's first opera tells the story of Orpheus. Orfeo, first produced at Mantua in 1607 and still a popular piece today, broke new ground as a 'musical drama' in which the music was an integral and expressive part of the story.

The tale of Orpheus fascinated opera composers – partly perhaps because Orpheus himself was a musician, but also (as with Monteverdi) because the story tells an ancient Mystery and therefore has immense power. Between 1600 and 2005 no fewer than 66 versions were written. Gluck's version of 1762 restores the most ancient ending, bringing Eurydice back to life to be happily reunited with Orpheus.

Not only was Greek theatre dedicated to Dionysus, but also both the Eleusinian and Orphic Mysteries included powerfully dramatic elements. The splendid age of Elizabethan and Jacobean theatre and the rise of opera ensured that the Mysteries would still be staged, although this time for an audience of spectators rather than participants. We can hardly speculate whether any of the audience recognized consciously what was occurring during a production, or whether any of the actors deliberately worked to evoke the Mysteries. However, as has been noted, the power of the Mysteries is such that participation ensures a deep experience of the Divine. To a lesser degree this can still be true of theatre and opera even today, and actors still speak of the 'blessing' that they sometimes feel when playing Shakespeare.

The survival of the tale of Orpheus is remarkable in itself and proof of an enduring power. If we absorb ourselves in the power of the music, we may still enjoy a taste of what the ancient initiations felt like. Watching or participating in a production of *The Tempest* or Monteverdi's *Orfeo* or Gluck's *Orfeo ed Euridice* can take us right back to the world of the earliest of the Greeks who were initiated into the Mysteries of life and death.

THE GOLD MAKERS

JOHN DEE LIVED AT A TIME when the very nature of the way the world was viewed was changing. During the next two centuries magic would remain as an integral part of people's worldview, but there was also an increasing interest in practical, experimental science. Nor were the two seen as antithetical: quite the opposite. The innovators who brought about the scientific revolution were themselves skilled in astrology and alchemy. But later generations of scientists felt a need to distance themselves from magical and philosophical thinking, thereby limiting the sphere of science to physical reality and altogether discounting its spiritual potential.

> The outer sun hungers for the inner sun.
> — Jakob Böhme, *De Signatura Rerum*

THE AGE OF GOLD

The art of alchemy has been practised since around the third century BCE, and alchemists have flourished in Egypt, China and the Islamic world as well as Europe. The greatest flowering in the West was during the sixteenth and seventeenth centuries. Both the revival of classical learning that had sparked the Renaissance and the invention of printing contributed towards an enriching of the art, making esoteric texts more freely available. However, alchemy by its very nature was not open to all. An alchemist had to have considerable quantities of time and money to spare, and he also needed to be educated to a reasonable level.

Alchemy is a bizarre and extraordinarily demanding pursuit, requiring absolute concentration and devotion for an unpredictable length of time. Nor is success guaranteed, yet it can appear so close as to lure the practitioner onwards until the end of his days. No wonder there are so many stories of alchemists ruining their fortunes and their health! Not only are the alchemical texts too obscure to be penetrated without a highly developed intuition as well as years of study, but also the practical work is physically dangerous. Some substances used – for example mercury – are poisonous, and there is always the danger of explosion or other accident. It used to be believed that the philosopher's stone would be achieved only by those destined to do so, and the aspiring alchemist was advised to study his horoscope for signs of success. Beyond doubt many practitioners have over the centuries been driven to distraction and some perhaps even to insanity. For their pains they have become the butt of jokes, though they are engaged in a deadly serious business.

Alchemists made many significant discoveries during the course of their work, some of which can be related to modern science and some not. For example, distillation is an important part of the alchemical work, and it is said that an alchemist was the first to distil brandy. He thought at first that he had achieved the elixir of life itself! But despite alchemy's appearance of being the forerunner of experimental science, the alchemical world-view is a mystical one. Alchemists believe that the material world contains a spiritual reality, so that it is the destiny not only of mankind but also of the whole cosmos to return to the perfection of its divine maker. The symbol of this process is the ouroboros, the snake that eats its own tail – a paradoxical image typical of alchemy, but implying that eventually material reality will be sublimated into spiritual unity.

The process of alchemy is to begin with a base material and by various chemical means purify it until it becomes the 'philosopher's stone' that can turn metals to gold. Gold is emblematic of the most perfect metal due to its extraordinary properties. In esoteric terms, it is associated with the Sun, the symbol of highest divinity and also of Apollo. Since the orbit of the planet Mercury is nearest to the Sun, the two are considered to be related, just as Mercury and Apollo are brothers in Greek mythology. The spirit Mercurius, who is the alchemist's guide, will lead him to the achievement of the Sun, the true gold of spirituality.

The language used in alchemical manuals reflects very vividly that of the Mysteries. The base substance is required to be metaphorically 'killed' in order to reveal its true life, just like the initiate at Eleusis undergoing an experience of death while still alive. Indeed, alchemy conceals the knowledge of the Mysteries. Where it is unusual is that it produces physical changes in a chemical substance as well as spiritual purification in the alchemist himself.

Some alchemists were certainly in it for the money, but others were aware of the true value of the work. Writing in the seventeenth century, Pierre-Jean Fabre defined the process thus:

> Alchemy is not merely an art or science to teach metallic transmutation, so much as a true and solid science that teaches how to know the centre of all things, which in the divine language is called the Spirit of Life.
> (Rola, p.8)

In other words, alchemy is an esoteric way of penetrating to the very core of life, of discovering that the spirit animating the natural world of herbs, plants and metals is identical with that of human beings. The alchemist who experiences this finds his life has also, in some sense, turned to gold.

ALCHEMY AS MEDICINE

One of the most influential alchemists of all times practised the art not for gold but rather for medicine. Paracelsus (1493–1541) was an extrovert, opinionated and controversial figure. After qualifying as a doctor in Vienna, he wandered through Europe and further afield to Africa and Asia pursuing his practice and seeking out wisdom from hidden sources. With Paracelsus we find the first magus who operates both in the magical realm and what we now see as the strictly physical world, for he introduced the use of chemicals into medicine which up to that point had been entirely herbal. Yet Paracelsus followed Ficino's ideas closely. He developed Ficino's teachings on using stones, herbs, scents and food to attract planetary influences. Like Ficino, Paracelsus believed that health arises when a person achieves a state of harmonious balance with the universe, and to this end he practised alchemy. His aim, though, was to find medicinal substances rather than to reach the Divine or to become rich.

Paracelsus was a truly original thinker who accepted no ideas at face value. He believed that the Divine infuses the whole of creation to the extent that creation is God. This heretical idea did not deter one of his more conventionally devout disciples, Heinrich Khunrath (c.1560–1605), who developed a Christian alchemy with the express purpose of uniting himself to the Divine.

Khunrath was also a well-travelled medical man. While in Prague he met and was profoundly impressed by Dee. He may have learned his alchemy from Dee and Kelley and we remember that Dee conducted his angelic conversations with prayers and Christian piety, living by his assertion that the 'key of Prayer openeth all things' (French, p.116). Khunrath, though, followed Paracelsus in believing that practical experiment should take equal place with prayer. His motto *Ora et labora* – prayer and work – became a celebrated saying among alchemists.

Alchemists such as these worked in a harmonious way, integrating spiritual and physical forces in the tradition of Ficino. Their knowledge was based on the ancient sources we have studied and their aims were the same as those of the Greek Mysteries: to achieve harmony and to penetrate the realm of the Divine. Alchemy itself was seen as a Mystery: it revealed the presence of divinity in the humblest of natural substances. This is the background from which our modern, secular science sprang. But during this period there were other channels through which the hidden wisdom flowed.

THE FREEMASON AND HIS KING

Even in England, where he had been forced to end his days in poverty, Dee continued to have his admirers. One of the most celebrated is Elias Ashmole (1617–92), the founder of the first public museum: the Ashmolean in Oxford. Ashmole was known as 'the English Merlin' and his interests covered a multitude of subjects. He was an antiquarian and an avid collector; he wrote a highly praised history of the Order of the Garter; he studied heraldry, history, genealogy and medicine. Ashmole lived by astrology, using it with some success to choose a wealthy wife and even advising Charles II at tricky political moments. What's more,

The Mysteries of Freemasonry are founded on the building of the Temple of Solomon in which the Ark was housed.

he studied alchemy with a certain William Backhouse, who reputedly revealed to him the secret of the philosopher's stone on his deathbed. Although Ashmole had already published several books on alchemy, after that moment he remained silent on the subject.

Ashmole lived through the turbulent events of the Civil War, the execution of Charles I, Cromwell's Protectorate and the restoration of the monarchy with Charles II. This critical period in English history in some ways reflects the turning point in the mystical arts. For instance, Charles II founded the Royal Society in 1660 with the aim of 'the promotion of Experimental learning' – but as well as supporting the development of scientific method, he had his own alchemical laboratory. Ashmole, like Charles, straddled the divide: he was one of the founder members of the Society, believing that the new, experimental methods of scientific enquiry could only benefit alchemy and astrology.

As well as being involved in the Royal Society, Ashmole is also a key figure in the development of the Freemasons. The origins of Freemasonry are coloured with myth. Symbolically the society is said to derive from the time of Solomon, who built a temple to house the Ark of the Covenant. The Knights Templar were said to have seized the Ark and enshrined Solomon's secrets in Masonic lore, although there is no firm evidence for this. As we have seen, the great Gothic cathedrals of Europe have been considered to embody alchemical secrets in their decoration and there are other theories about the builders (masons) encrypting knowledge in these sacred buildings. But Ashmole and his fellow Freemasons were not workers in stone but 'speculative' masons. Ashmole's note of his initiation in his diary on 16 October 1646 is almost the first record we have of Freemasonry, although a manuscript of a Masonic poem (*the Regius poem*), possibly composed in the late fourteenth century, is held in the British Library in London.

The symbolism of Freemasonry centres upon architecture, and figures familiar to us such as Pythagoras and Plato are revered for their mystical understanding of number and proportion. Freemasonry is organized as a Mystery: initiates preserve the secrets revealed to them as assiduously as those ancient Greeks who entered the temple at Eleusis. Yet, unlike the ancient Mystery cults, Freemasonry aimed at and achieved a large measure of power in the material and economic world. It was able to do this because it attracted wealthy and influential men, up to and including royalty. Indeed, right from its first real appearance during Ashmole's life it changed the course of history, for it seems that following the bloody violence of the Civil War and the Puritanical suppressions of the Commonwealth, the monarchy would never have been restored without Masonic help.

The key figure in the Restoration was General George Monck, whose secretiveness and subtlety made him an invaluable commander much in demand by both Commonwealth and Royalist parties. After Cromwell's death in 1658, his son Richard was unable to control the New Model Army and so it was possible for Charles Stuart to enter into secret negotiations with Monck, who was Governor of Scotland. Monck brought his army south and organized a new parliament packed with Royalists who voted to restore Charles to power.

What is astonishing is that both Monck and Charles were surrounded by Freemasons whose support and planning seem to have been crucial to the success of events. Freemasonry was a powerful force in Scotland, which was its earliest base in the British Isles. Negotiations were carried out clandestinely with Charles partly through the dashing and beautiful Elizabeth, Lady Dysart, who took as her second husband the Secretary of State for Scotland. Lady Dysart was well versed in arcane knowledge, including the making of invisible ink – a useful skill that she employed in Charles' service. She travelled frequently to the Continent on the pretence of family business and it is thought that she used Masonic symbolism to conceal messages for the King's party. The Scottish Freemasons were strongly Royalist in outlook and it is probable that Monck was himself a Mason, thus gaining access to a network of influential men throughout both Scotland and England.

When Charles II entered London on 29 May 1660, his 30th birthday, it was a triumph for the powers of Freemasonry. Ashmole celebrated Charles' arrival with a poem in which he compared the new king to the sun rising over London in Gemini, the city's own astrological sign. He seems to have hoped for great things from this alchemically inclined king: 'Tis a Time for Miracles to work' (Josten, Vol. 1, p.129).

But what does this political success say about the secret wisdom? Here it is at work in the most worldly of ways: the inner work, the ascent to Divinity, has been completely forgotten. Perhaps we already glimpsed the process of dilution with Elias Ashmole. Whereas Dee gained a reputation (to his cost) of being a powerful magician, Ashmole's knowledge of the arcane arts of alchemy and astrology was openly celebrated; he was admired but certainly not feared. The initiations of Freemasonry led not to visions of the spiritual world but to power in this one.

THE ROSY CROSS

At around the time Freemasonry was on the rise, another and even more mysterious society announced itself. Two pamphlets, published in 1614 and 1615, told the story of Father C. R. C., the founder of the Fraternity; a third pamphlet, *The Chemical Wedding of Christian Rosencreutz*, came out in 1616. As the title suggests, it uses alchemy in allegorical terms and Rosencreutz means 'rose cross'. These mysterious publications called for a universal reformation, a complete renewal of mankind, and invited those interested to join the Fraternity. Doing so was not, however, made easy, for the Rosicrucians did not divulge their whereabouts. All the same, this 'invisible college' with its mystical language and promises of purification inspired enormous interest across Europe.

The Rosicrucians seem to have been inspired by Dee, and in particular his *Monas Hieroglyphica*, in which he discusses the symbol of the cross. Dee's London Seal appears in the Chemical Wedding, which seems to draw directly upon his fervently pious attitude to magic. Although several societies calling themselves Rosicrucian sprang up much later (mostly in the nineteenth and twentieth centuries), the identity of the original Rosicrucians remains a total mystery. Their symbolism and outlook found its way into Freemasonry as well as alchemy and several alchemists – Ashmole and Khunrath amongst them – have been labelled Rosicrucians.

This most mysterious of all secret societies – so mysterious that its very existence has never been proved – brings back into the picture the true purpose of the secret wisdom. The Rosicrucians aimed high, for they wanted nothing less than a complete renovation of the arts, politics, philosophy and religion. The pamphlets suggest that the only way to achieve those aims is through individual transformation, a purification of soul to reveal its inherent divinity that is the real aim of alchemy. We are back in the world of the ancient Mysteries, only this time envisaged on a continent-wide scale.

Meanwhile, in laboratories throughout Europe men practising astrology and alchemy were also making earth-shattering discoveries that led to the old world of magic being smothered by material reality. The last magicians were about to become the first 'men of reason'.

THE TEMPLE OF THE WORLD

Now we have looked at the mingling of mystical influences on the development of science, let us take a closer look at the men who made it happen. The first of these rearranged the order of the entire universe, when Nicolaus Copernicus (1473–1543) published his theory that the sun rather than the earth stands at the centre of the solar system. Copernicus' discovery not only altered the placing of the planets, it also revealed the universe to be of a different nature than had been thought. For, as we have seen, the common understanding was that the earth represented the furthest point from God and heaven, with the spheres of the elements and planets forming concentric circles in between. The whole system was symbolic, with heaven being perfect, the fixed stars eternal and the earth representing the heaviest, least perfect, part of the universal scheme.

Yet Copernicus and his contemporaries seem to have been able to retain their faith in a divinely appointed universe far better than did the Church. Symbolic reality remained in place for them, alongside the new understanding of the material facts of the universe. Urged on by friends and colleagues, Copernicus took a momentous step in the history of science and put forward the heliocentric theory in 1543, but in the introductory paragraph of his book *De Revolutionibus Orbium Coelestium* he lauded the spiritual nature of the heavens' 'transcendent perfection', calling the cosmos 'a visible god' (Copernicus, *Book 1*, Introduction). In this he echoes, perhaps consciously, one of the most celebrated Orphic fragments on the universal nature of Zeus:

Would you behold his head and his fair face,
It is the resplendent heaven, round which his golden locks
Of glittering stars are beautifully exalted in the air...
His eyes the sun and the opposing moon.
(Cory, p.290)

Copernicus goes on to praise the usefulness of the art 'labelled astronomy by some, astrology by others', using Plato as his revered source. It is quite clear that he considers this knowledge to be of the sort that properly belongs to a magus as defined by Pico, for he states that Plato considers it 'highly unlikely that anyone lacking the requisite knowledge of the sun, moon, and other heavenly bodies can become and be called godlike' (Copernicus, *Book 1*, Ch. 8).

Surprisingly, his *De Revolutionibus Orbium Coelestium* did not even attract much notice when it was published, let alone controversy. Perhaps one reason for the general lack of shock at Copernicus' theory could be that he allowed the earth its symbolic place, stating that 'the ancients insist that the earth remains at rest in the middle of the universe, and that this is its status is beyond any doubt' (Copernicus, *Book 1*, Introduction). Copernicus himself was a deeply religious man and indeed the concept of a universe that was neither divinely created nor constantly guided by God would be very difficult to hold at this period.

Nor did Copernicus' Christian beliefs prevent him from examining the work of the Neopythagorean astronomers who were the very first people in the Western world to put forward the idea of heliocentricity. So he is drawing on mystical sources and indeed mentions Pythagoras by name.

In Chapter Ten of *De Revolutionibus* Copernicus presents a diagram of the solar system with the planets in their correct physical order, rather than in the traditional Ptolemaic order. He lists the length of orbits of each before turning his attention to the sun. And at this point – the most important moment of his exposition – he reveals himself as deeply indebted to the ancient wisdom. Copernicus is very far from seeing the universe in mechanical terms: for him, as for Orpheus, the sun is a deity:

> In the centre of all rests the sun. For who would place this lamp of a very beautiful temple in another or better place than this wherefrom it can illuminate everything at the same time? As a matter of fact, not unhappily do some call it lantern; others, the mind and still others, the pilot of the world. Trismegistus calls it a 'visible god'.
>
> (French, p.102)

John Dee was twenty-six when Copernicus published his theory and must have been familiar with it: in the *Monas Hieroglyphica* he gives absolute importance to the sun. In a way, heliocentricity validates what the mystic philosophers already knew, merely adding proof of the sun's physical centrality to its symbolic supremacy.

A HERETICAL SCIENTIST

The first person to espouse Copernican theory – and get into deep trouble for doing so – was Galileo Galilei (1564–1642). He seems to have learned from his father, a musician, the basic Pythagorean understanding linking musical notes with mathematical proportions. Galileo was also an astrologer but although he was undoubtedly competent at calculating horoscopes, his interpretative skill was not highly developed and he sometimes applied to friends for help.

However, it was his scientific thought rather than his astrological peering into the future that led the Inquisition in Rome to censure him in 1616 and then to try him for heresy in 1633. Galileo was made to deny that the sun lay at the centre of the solar system, since such an idea opposed Holy Scripture. Legend has it that he defiantly muttered, 'And yet it moves', and certainly he must have been thinking that. Galileo remained under house arrest for the rest of his life and, incredibly, the Vatican only conceded that his views were correct in 1992.

Galileo had studied the laws of motion and used a new invention, the telescope, with which he was the first to observe three of the moons of Jupiter. Here we find astrology entering the picture again. Galileo published his discovery in a short work called *Sidereus Nuncius* – The Starry Messenger. Dedicating the book to Grand Duke Cosimo II of Tuscany, Galileo opened it with an eloquent account of Jupiter in Cosimo's horoscope. Since Jupiter is the planet ruling generosity and protection, this is a clever move to appeal to those qualities in Cosimo – who did, in fact, become his patron. But it also demonstrates that Galileo was far from being the pure scientist that he is often made out to be. In fact, his library contained a good selection of works on the occult philosophy and astrology – about 24 books plus 21 ephemerides (tables for calculating horoscopes).

MUSIC OF THE SPHERES

Astronomers at this period can hardly have looked at the heavens without a sense of awe that it would be natural to interpret in terms of religion. As we have seen, for Copernicus the sun was nothing less than a god. What's more, the use of mathematics was still considered virtually magical. But why were the astronomers so keen to study the movements of the heavens in the first place? In the case of Tycho Brahe (1546–1601), it was because he wanted to increase the accuracy of astrological predictions. The astronomical tables then in use (the Alphonsine Tables) were far from accurate, which is hardly surprising. The Ptolemaic order of the planets could not be used to predict the planets' movements since it was largely wrong. Unfortunately, Copernicus' theory did not much improve matters because he was still imagining the universe to be a vision of perfection and thus thought the planets moved in flawlessly circular orbits.

Tycho aimed to refine and perfect astronomical calculations to produce more accurate planetary tables. His interest was personal, for he was not only a celebrated astronomer but also an astrologer and alchemist. Two of his royal patrons – Frederick II of Denmark and Rudolph II the Holy Roman Emperor – consulted him for predictions. Tycho conformed to the views of his astrological forbears such as Ficino by believing that astrology was a complex art beyond the scope of any but learned men:

Galileo's observation of the moons of Jupiter inspired him to describe his patron Cosimo II's horoscope.

he stated that he 'did not consider astrology a delusive science when it is kept within bounds and not abused by ignorant people' (Schofield).

In 1572 Tycho observed a new star in the constellation of Cassiopeia. This was not supposed to happen, since everything above the moon – from planets to stars – was believed to be immutable. Tycho's discovery delivered a second blow to the ancient world-view. If the upper regions of the universe were not perfect and eternal as had been thought, where was the Divine? Then in 1577 a comet appeared – traditionally an omen of great change in society. Tycho produced astrological predictions accordingly, but he also carried out mathematical calculations that proved the comet to be above the moon, in the supposedly eternally changeless region of the heavens. Astronomy, rather than making man godlike, was beginning to alter man's perception of God and his creation.

Both Frederick II of Sweden and Rudolph II were immensely generous to Tycho, allowing him to build fabulous observatories and alchemical laboratories. These two disciplines are linked, since the progress of alchemical work depends upon utilizing planetary influences at appropriate times. Tycho must have hoped that his more accurate observations would greatly assist his alchemical studies, but these remain mysterious. Although he enjoyed immense wealth, he inherited much of that from his parents. Whether he augmented it by alchemical means is unknown.

THE HARMONY OF THE WORLD

Mysticism is an integral part of the history of the development of astrology. Tycho's most celebrated pupil, the great Johannes Kepler (1571–1630), sought to restore the sense of perfection to the universe, although he is not often remembered for that aspect of his work. Kepler grew up in the care of his mother, who seems to have practised magic and herbal healing, since she was at one point accused of witchcraft. When Kepler was six she took him out one night to a hill, from which vantage point they observed the 1577 comet. That memorable night seems to have made such an impression on Kepler that he developed a passion for astronomy. Working his way up through school and university, where he studied theology, he developed a talent for mathematics and astrology. These interests underpinned his work on astronomy, and his first work is profoundly mystical in tone. *The Mysterium Cosmographicum* or Cosmographic Mystery (1596) declares its viewpoint in the title. It is a Mystery – for Kepler believed that he had discovered, in an inspired moment, the plan on which God had built the universe.

What was this plan? Kepler took on board Copernicus' theory of heliocentricity but worked it out through Pythagorean theories of proportion. He claimed that the planetary spheres could be measured in terms of the five perfect geometric solids, known as the Platonic solids, surrounded by a sphere representing Saturn's orbit. He then applied these proportions to musical harmonic intervals, believing he had achieved what Ficino had found so hard – putting into musical notation the sound of each planet as it orbited. Harmony, to Kepler, was his 'theory of everything'. He went on to apply the Platonic proportions to astrological aspects (the distances measured between planets as they move). This last aspect of his work produced three new aspects that are still used by astrologers today.

Pattern and order fascinated Kepler: everywhere in nature he saw the handiwork of the Divine. He wrote on snowflakes, comparing their hexagonal shape to honeycombs. God, he said, had imprinted bees with the instinct to build that eminently practical shape. He believed that pomegranates grow in response to the soul of their tree. Kepler, like Ficino, strove to see the relationships that link the cosmos together. He too was attempting to unify his soul with the Divine through contemplating the natural world, and he too saw the sun as a visible deity, orchestrating the surrounding universe in the music of the spheres.

During the last year of Tycho's life, Kepler worked briefly as his assistant and enjoyed his financial support. He benefited hugely from Tycho's determination to improve the accuracy of astronomical calculations and his willingness to throw aside millennia of belief in favour of empirical evidence – to say nothing of his appropriation of Tycho's notes after his death. Kepler began to make a detailed study of the orbit of Mars, using Tycho's calculations as his starting point. But this apparently empirical study was all a part of his desire to refine the proofs for his Platonic universe, and as such very far from being 'pure' science in the modern sense of the term. Eventually, in 1619, Kepler brought out his *Harmonices Mundi* or Harmony of the World, the culmination of his vision of the universe as geometrically constructed by God according to Plato's description in *Timaeus*. In a way this is the last great cry of Pythagoreanism. Thus it is ironic that in the book Kepler presents his laws of planetary motion, which were to be taken up by Newton and used as evidence for the mechanical, soulless nature of the universe.

Amazingly, though, this great book was not Kepler's last, nor was it considered his masterpiece. That accolade was claimed by his new, improved ephemerides for astrologers, dedicated to the Emperor Rudolph II – *the Rudolphine Tables*. With Kepler we find for the last time the highest achievements in astronomy comfortably married to astrology. The universe is still seen as mysterious and divine, it is still alive and imbued with a soul – it just begins to be a little more predictable. And prediction has always been the aim of astrology.

THE SECRET ALCHEMIST

Copernicus, Tycho and Kepler all referred to astronomy/astrology as an art. Sir Isaac Newton too continued in that tradition, regarding himself as a 'natural philosopher'. But with Newton and his discoveries we move inexorably away from the ancient view of the animated, divine universe and towards the modern view.

Isaac Newton (1643–1727) was born into a world in which the magical thought underlying the work of earlier astronomers was dying out. In its place was an ambition to learn about nature in order to control it. Man as magus was turning his divine powers in a more materialistic direction. However, Newton himself still retained an aura of mystery. A profoundly religious man, he practised alchemy with enthusiasm and determination. Indeed, mercury poisoning – a common cause of illness and death amongst alchemists – may have caused Newton's increasing eccentricity later in life and even his death. His executors suppressed his mass of alchemical books and notes and they did not surface again until 1936, when they caused a sensation. The economist John Maynard Keynes bought the papers and announced Newton to be 'the last of the magicians' (Keynes, pp.363–40).

During his life Newton seems to have kept his alchemy quiet; he was very protective of his reputation and may have feared that he would attract ridicule. We are now entering a world in which the secret wisdom would increasingly be hidden, not so much to keep it from falling into the wrong hands but because it was no longer valued. However, Newton's interest in alchemy was hardly surprising, since at Cambridge University he studied Copernicus and Kepler with enthusiasm. Newton still believed that occult – in the sense of hidden – forces were active in the universe, and it has been said that had he not been influenced by occult ideas about action at a distance he would not have developed his theory of gravity. Newton was the first to show that white light refracts into a rainbow of colours, which he classified as seven because it is a potent number in magic.

Newton's reputation as the most influential person in the history of science rests upon his great opus *Philosophiae Naturalis Principia Mathematica* (1687) or the Natural History of Mathematical Principles, usually known simply as the *Principia*. In this work, Newton used Kepler's laws of planetary motion in conjunction with his own theory of gravity to arrive at universal laws of motion. In doing so he turned the universe into a predictable machine, although he himself resisted such a view. But the damage had been done: now that forces within the universe could be described by logical mathematical arguments, the mystery of divinity retreated out of reach. Instead of the planets showering down rays connecting stones, plants, animals and people in chains of similarity, the universe held together with a single, neutral force: gravity. The spiritual concept of love as the unifying universal power was replaced by the physical principle of weight. In astrological terms, the celestial Venus was ousted by Saturn, the ruler of material reality – and melancholy.

Where now would a magician begin his climb up the Ladder of Being to the final goal of divinity? The rungs had been broken; spirit had been banished from matter. No longer did the planetary angels sing in harmony as they whirled through space, nor did arriving and departing souls pass through their spheres on their way to and from the imperfect earth. No place in the universe was any longer more or less perfect than any other. So why did Newton continue to practise alchemy? In this area of his life at least he must have entered into spiritual realms of transformation. It has been rumoured that the pursuit of alchemy caused him to have a nervous breakdown, but perhaps it was the tension between his occult and public studies that briefly destroyed his equilibrium.

Newton's discoveries mark the point at which astronomy leaves the realm of the arts and is claimed by science. From now on, the discipline of science claims the material world and leaves the spiritual to religion, as well as to magicians and alchemists. It is as if the universe, which Plato and Ficino loved as a divine being imbued with soul by its creator, has died. Gold has become lead.

William Blake depicts Newton measuring the world, rather like a follower of Pythagoras.

SUBLIME
RHYME

WHILE ASTROLOGERS and alchemists were busying themselves unwittingly creating the new discipline of science, the secret wisdom found other ways to survive. True to the spirit of Orpheus, it emerged through poetry and poetic prose. Some of the writers were profoundly religious men; at least one had an intimate knowledge of alchemy; several were well read in the Neoplatonic tradition. And as time passes, we shall see that the boundaries between science and the imagination were far from being as rigid as they are today.

> To see a World in a Grain of Sand
> And a Heaven in a Wild Flower,
> Hold Infinity in the palm of your hand
> And Eternity in an hour.
> — William Blake,
> *Auguries of Innocence*

KEEPERS OF THE FLAME

When Elizabeth I visited John Dee at Mortlake in order to be instructed in his mystical work *Monas Hieroglyphica*, she was pursuing an interest in hidden knowledge that pervaded her court. During her reign she and her courtiers deliberately cultivated an atmosphere of mystery and magic in which she became the Faery Queen, her political power enhanced by mystical strength. Courtiers vied with each other to praise her in extravagant terms, elevating her to the status of a goddess. While this fantasizing had sound political motives, some of the poets who vied for the Queen's somewhat capricious favour were employing their knowledge of Neoplatonism to find themes for verse. After all, Plato himself wrote of an ideal ruler who would be a philosopher capable of guiding society wisely: Elizabeth could be seen as such a queen. Edmund Spenser (c.1552–99) celebrated her as Gloriana in his epic fantasy poem *The Faerie Queene*, in which he used the chivalrous adventures of a group of knights in a magical setting to illustrate various virtues.

Other poets wrote more personally. The romantic and glamorous Sir Philip Sidney (1554–86) employed the Platonic idea of love in his poetry as a clever means of praising his beloved, claiming to find the highest spiritual beauty in physical form. Neither the overtly political aims of Spenser's poem nor the courtly elegance of Sidney's can be seen as doing anything other than playing lightly for literary effect with the profound insights of the ancient world – and yet, the magic worked upon Sidney. Primarily a love poet, he crowned his verse (and, perhaps, his short life) with a sonnet declaring his understanding of his own divine nature and his desire to return to the source of love. 'Leave me, O love which reachest but to dust', he commands, turning his soul instead towards the spiritual light of the sun:

> Which breaks the clouds and opens forth the light
> That doth both shine and give us light to see.
> O take fast hold; let that light be thy guide...
> Then farewell, world! thy uttermost I see:
> Eternal Love, maintain thy life in me.
>
> (Bullett, p.278)

The piety that both Spenser and Sidney show, with their emphasis on moral virtues, may seem rather distant from the intense spiritual explorations of the Mysteries. Certainly they are by no means so deeply involved in occult life as John Dee, but there is a link. Surprisingly, that link is Christian piety expressed through Puritanism. The word Puritan probably conjures up images of grim-faced men in black clothes doing their best to crush all worldly pleasures – a legacy of Cromwell's time. But Sidney was a Puritan and Dee, as we have seen, performed his angel magic in a state of almost constant prayer. At this period, Puritanism held out the hope of universal reform – a dream and aspiration that was shared by the mysterious Rosicrucians. So this religious movement embraces the insights of the ancient world and interprets them anew.

A POET AND CLERIC

As we know, the initiatory knowledge of the Mysteries passed into alchemy to create a discipline that aimed at purifying not just human beings but the whole world. And alchemical symbolism too finds its place in poetry at this time. One of the greatest poets of this period, John Donne (1572–1631) lived a colourful life. Born a Catholic, he converted to Anglicanism and rose to become Dean of St Paul's – pausing often along the way to enjoy the company of a number of women besides his wife. His poetry is equally passionate on the delights of physical love and on his profound sense of unworthiness before God, and for both themes he uses a wealth of alchemical symbolism. Not only that, but he delivered lengthy sermons (often to a congregation including many swooning women) in which he developed intricate alchemical allegories to explain the mysteries of Christianity.

Like Ficino, Donne combined quite effortlessly a Hermetic understanding with his Christian belief. He describes himself as a microcosm in best alchemical style:

> I am a little world made cunningly
> Of elements, and an angelic sprite.
> (*Divine Meditations*, Smith, p.310)

The 'sprite' is his guardian angel or daimon, his proof that he is inwardly divine, although he has fallen from God's grace to which he now aspires again.

Donne's secular love poetry is rightly celebrated as among the most sensual and vivid in the English language. In The Ecstasy he describes two lovers lying on a violet-covered bank, finding that holding hands and looking into each other's eyes brings them to a state of bliss greater than that of sexual love. Their souls mingle, revealing to them one of the first stages in Socrates' ladder of love: the realization of the beloved's spiritual beauty. However, rather than rising higher towards the contemplation of divine love, Donne's lovers argue for the virtue of bodies to bring this spiritual love into the material world:

> Loves' mysteries in souls do grow,
> But yet the body is his book.
>
> (*The Ecstasy*, Smith, p.55)

While it could be said that Donne, Sidney and Spenser are playing with mystical imagery rather than experiencing it with the aim of uniting themselves more closely with divinity, it remains true that their poetry protected vestiges of the hidden wisdom and ensured its survival. Other poets, such as Henry Vaughan (1621–95), experienced the mysteries of alchemy first hand.

ALCHEMICAL TWINS

Vaughan, like Donne, is known as a metaphysical poet: one whose poetry is characterized by elaborate and arcane metaphors and inventive language. His early poetry is unremarkable, but some time shortly before 1650 he almost died from an illness that he interpreted as a punishment for his worldly ways and a warning to purify his life. He adopted the motto moriendo revixi – 'through dying, I regenerate' – an insight straight out of the Mysteries and Hermes Trismegistus. Vaughan's next collection of poetry, *Silex Scintillans* (The Sparkling Stone), reflects his observation that 'the way up is the way down': 'Certaine Divine Raies breake out of the Soul in adversity, like sparks of fire out of the afflicted flint' (Gardner, p.321). But the title also suggests the philosopher's stone – and that is no accident, for Henry's twin brother Thomas (1621–66) was a famous alchemist.

The poetry in *Silex Scintillans* focuses on the purity of childhood and the adult's fallen state. Vaughan knows by experience what is needed to regain that state of 'Angel-infancy': a poem called Regeneration ends with the heartfelt cry:

> Lord, then said I, On me one breath,
> And let me dye before my death!
>
> (Gardner, p.264)

Elsewhere, he confides almost casually a mystical vision:
I saw Eternity the other night
Like a great Ring of pure and endless light.

(Gardner, p.271)

After contrasting the beauty and light of divine life with the 'vast shadow' that envelops the world, Vaughan dismisses all worldly pursuits as bringing nothing but 'blood and tears'. He praises those who find their wings (like the wings sprouted by the lover in Plato's Banquet) to fly upwards along:

The way which from this dead and dark abode Leads up to God,
A way where you might tread the Sun, and be More bright than he.

(Gardner, p.272)

Through being brought close to death, Henry Vaughan seems to have experienced a spiritual regeneration that he saw in the traditional terms of the hidden wisdom, although in his poetry he expressed it in Christian terminology. His intimate understanding of esoteric knowledge is beyond doubt. His brother Thomas, the alchemist, was trained as a doctor and concentrated on making medicinal substances, following Paracelsus closely. He also wrote under the pseudonym Eugenius Philalethes, producing alchemical tracts in which he mentions or quotes Orpheus, the Pythagoreans, the Kabbalah, the Chaldean Oracles and the Corpus Hermeticum. Delightfully, Vaughan offers some medicines that are so easy to prepare, he claims, that a lady can do the work while simultaneously reading Sir Philip Sidney's poetry! And it is a fact that he and his wife Rebecca performed alchemy as a couple, reflecting in their own marriage the alchemical mystic marriage of opposites.

Thomas Vaughan enlivens some of his alchemical works with poetry, showing less genius than his brother but underlining the suitability of verse for expressing, concisely and in vivid imagery, the mystical essence of alchemy. The poetic imagination moves easily in the world of the esoteric, intuitively understanding truths that scientists refuse to accept without proof. While the Vaughan twins lived at a time when the split between science and the arts (and religion) was only just beginning to happen, the vital role of poetry in carrying the hidden wisdom will become increasingly clear as we look at later poets.

THE PLATONIC PURITAN

With the poetry of John Milton (1608–74), we move deeper into the world of the Mysteries. Milton, a passionate and extraordinarily learned man, wrote little that can be considered light reading: his poetry expressed both the depth of his beliefs and the breadth of his knowledge. Born in London to a father who had converted from Catholicism to Anglicanism, Milton was a precocious and hard-working genius. Religion was clearly an extremely important influence upon him, but to his Puritan spirituality he added the fruits of a Cambridge education followed by six years of solitary learning and travelling widely on the Continent. Part of Milton's extraordinary fascination lies in his versatility: when not composing majestic verse he was busy writing powerful political tracts upholding the ideals of Cromwell's Republic – so much so that he had to go into hiding for a while at the Restoration.

However, what interests us is the poetry and its mystical aspects that belie Milton's image as a severe Puritan. During his travels in Italy he was fêted at several academies and some of his early poems, written before he went abroad, show that he must have known Ficino's work quite intimately. In 1631, when he was only 23, Milton wrote two poems designed to be read as a pair: *L'Allegro* (The Happy One) and *Il Penseroso* (The Thoughtful One). The poems illustrate exactly Ficino's theory of the necessity of balancing the serious side of life (study, contemplation) with more cheerful pleasures in order to align oneself with cosmic harmony.

L'Allegro banishes 'loathed Melancholy' and in its place evokes the pleasures of Venus and Bacchus, who bring in their train dances, jokes, songs, amorous delights and good food and drink (as this is set in England, Bacchus provides not wine but 'Spicy Nut-brown Ale'). Milton ends by evoking Orpheus himself, waking from his sleep on a bed of flowers to hear:

Such strains as would have won the ear
Of Pluto, to have quite set free
His half regained Eurydice.

(Wright, p.33)

This frothy and celebratory poem lists many of Ficino's recommended remedies against melancholy. But when we turn to *Il Penseroso* we find that Milton, like Ficino, sees cheerfulness not as an aim in itself but as a relief from the far more significant state of melancholy. Sadness has a valuable purpose and a hidden gift, and the poem makes it quite clear that Milton aspires to the spiritual insights that only the melancholy mood can offer. While joys are 'vain, deluding...toys', Melancholy is hailed as the divine daughter of Saturn. Pleasure can only connect us with this material world, whereas Melancholy 'rapt... in holy passion' allows us to rise heavenwards until we can hear:

> The Muses in a ring
> Ay round about Jove's altar sing.
>
> (Wright, p.35)

Whereas *L'Allegro* describes a sun-soaked summer countryside crowded with cheerful shepherds, *Il Penseroso* summons up a magical nightscape populated by gods, nymphs and mythical beings including various nature spirits and even Orpheus himself. Here, the poet stargazes in a lonely tower:

> Where I may oft outwatch the Bear,
> With thrice great Hermes, or unsphear
> The spirit of Plato to unfold
> What worlds, or what vast Regions hold
> Th'immortal mind that hath forsook
> His mansion in this fleshly nook:
> And of those Daemons that are found
> In fire, air, flood, or under ground,
> Whose power hath a true consent
> With Planet or with Element.
>
> (Wright, p.35–6)

This extraordinary profession of faith in Hermes Trismegistus and Plato marks Milton, for all his Puritanism, as a carrier of the ancient wisdom. In this poem too he evokes Orpheus, but this time he hints at the esoteric version of the story of Eurydice, describing Orpheus as singing so sweetly that Pluto grants him his wife back. The climax of the poem comes with a vision of Milton as an aged magician whose esoteric studies have developed him into a prophet:

And may at last my weary age
Find out the peaceful hermitage...
Where I might sit and rightly spell
Of every Star that Heav'n doth shew,
And every Herb that sips the dew;
Till old experience do attain
To something like Prophetic strain.

(Wright, p.37)

Il Penseroso proved to be an extraordinarily influential poem, inspiring later poets such as Blake and Yeats as well as artists such as Samuel Palmer. It is one of the conduits through which the hidden wisdom was carried onwards until with Yeats – who took the poem as a blueprint for life – it flowed into the channel of ritual magic.

THE FALL FROM GRACE

Even Milton's great Christian epic, *Paradise Lost*, includes echoes of occult Pagan knowledge. In Book 7 the angel Raphael relates, at Adam's request, the creation of the world – but he does so in alchemical terms. God treats the chaotic base material just as an alchemist would, subjecting it to separations, distillations, fermentations and the other means of purification until it achieves perfection. The message of this Christian alchemy is clear: when Man falls from grace he ruins the perfection of the world, which cannot be restored until Christ's advent.

What's more, Raphael – an angel seemingly well versed in hidden wisdom – expounds to Adam Diotima's ladder of love from Plato's *Symposium*. Adam confesses the passion that Eve arouses in him, only to be met with a frowning angel exhorting him to value not the lust that even animals feel but the superior delights of reason. For love:

... is the scale
By which to heav'nly Love thou mayst ascend.
(Wright, p.304)

Not for nothing did William Blake, who revered Milton, yet say memorably of him that he was 'of the Devil's party without knowing it'

SVS RAPHAEL
ARCHANGELVS

*Even the angels are Platonists. In Paradise Lost, Raphael flies down to
teach Adam about Diotima's ladder of love.*

(Keynes, p.50). Blake's Satan is the principle of life and energy, opposed to a repressive God. And true life, as Blake saw it, lies in the truths expressed in the ancient wisdoms – as we shall shortly see.

A SCIENTIST IN HEAVEN

Although the poets discussed above all kept the flame of the hidden wisdom burning through their verse, none of them (as far as we know) followed the ancient ways of meditation as a means of unity with the Divine. Henry Vaughan did, it is true, suffer an experience of coming close to death and his consequent spiritual rebirth made him into a true poet; but that was involuntary. Now we turn to a man who not only profoundly influenced later generations of poets but who travelled freely in the spiritual dimension. This man was not a poet or artist but a scientist, and in this he links together the worlds of Kepler and Newton with that of the poets.

Emanuel Swedenborg (1688–1772) has been described as one of the most remarkable men in history. Born in Sweden to a family whose considerable wealth came from mining, Swedenborg was deeply influenced by the somewhat unconventional religion that his father professed, but his education and first enthusiasm was for the sciences. His genius covered a broad range of subjects from mining to mathematics; he was also a keen inventor who was particularly proud of his designs for a flying machine. He knew enough to be able to make his own telescope and microscope; he is one of the founders of crystallography, and he was fluent in nine languages. Swedenborg was one of the last Renaissance men, his appetite for knowledge knowing no bounds and his ability to learn never failing him.

As Swedenborg explored the sciences, he turned increasingly towards the workings of the mind. He discovered the function of the cerebellum, but mechanical explanations of the brain failed to satisfy him. What he wanted to find was the seat of the soul. Swedenborg had practised breath control from an early age, so he was familiar with meditative technique. In 1744 he took a step towards being one of the forerunners of psychoanalysis by recording and interpreting his dreams. This led to a complete change in his life; he began to have visions, and his personality changed from being confident to the point of arrogance to being humble and modest.

The vision that was his introduction to the spiritual world might seem ridiculous to us, although it terrified him. It occurred when he was travelling in London. Habitually a frugal eater, he was for once enjoying a healthy appetite and was relishing a large tavern supper. All at once the room darkened and a man appeared in the corner, warning Swedenborg not to eat too much. Taking this literally, Swedenborg scurried straight back to his lodgings. However, it could be that the mysterious man was warning Swedenborg that his voluminous studies should draw to a close, which is in fact what happened.

That night, the man appeared in Swedenborg's dreams and explained that he was God and that Swedenborg had been chosen to 'explain to men the spiritual sense of the Scripture' (Dusen, p.60), an enterprise in which he would help. God then showed Swedenborg the spiritual worlds of heaven and hell. After that, Swedenborg's 'bodily eyes' were opened so that he saw the spiritual realms almost daily during his waking life. Swedenborg had undergone a regeneration, a death of his former self. He wrote: 'Regeneration takes place to the end that the life of the old man may die, and the new heavenly life be insinuated' (Synnestvedt, p.135).

EXPLORATIONS IN OTHER REALMS

Swedenborg devoted the rest of his life to following this Divine command and to exploring the realms of heaven and hell. In his writings he describes the nature of these realms in detail, fleshing out his visionary experience with hints given in the Scriptures. He seems to have experienced repeatedly the inner journey to the highest realms of being, just like Plotinus. Indeed, Swedenborg drew much inspiration from Plotinus and the Neoplatonists. Like them, he saw divinity as a spiritual sun that showers down influences to the lowest material realms. He laid great emphasis on the Chain of Being upon which Ficino built his magic, calling it the Law of Correspondences. He appreciated the spiritual content of the myths of antiquity and called magic and astrology the 'primary science of the ancients' (Dusen, p.170).

Just as for Socrates, Plato, Plotinus and Ficino, so for Swedenborg the one ruling principle of the universe is love. Man is lost if he does not live by this harmonious principle. After death, the soul is examined by angels and offered instruction. Every soul will follow its own nature, so souls willing to listen to the instruction will naturally pursue the angelic course to heaven, where all is harmony. Souls addicted to gross pleasures or evil will be drawn to the hell realms, where they are able to indulge themselves further. They are received there in a friendly manner by the damned, who are all too happy to see new sufferers recruited! But in heaven, souls engage themselves in furthering the cause of good in the world. Our whole earthly life is an initiation into the afterlife, and we carry the seeds of our future within us: 'Hell [is] in an evil man, and heaven in a good man' (Synnestvedt, p.105).

Swedenborg was certain from his own experience that he had found the universal truth, the wisdom common to all religions. The angels told him that religions are 'like so many jewels in a king's crown' (Dusen, p.222). Thus Swedenborg adopted a tolerant attitude, although he continued to think and see his visions in (unorthodox) Christian style and did not follow Proclus' example of worshipping gods from other religions.

Just as London was the setting for Swedenborg's experience of death and regeneration, so too it formed the backdrop for the end of his physical life. He travelled there in 1771 and fell ill shortly before Christmas, finally dying the following spring. The maid at his lodgings claimed that he knew early on that he was going to die and seemed delighted, 'as if he was going to have a holiday, to go to some merry-making' (Dusen, p.157). The afterlife could hold no surprises for him, so familiar was he with its landscape and inhabitants.

With Swedenborg we are back in the realm of the mystics who fully lived their convictions. His life was totally changed by his visions, just as the initiates at Eleusis reportedly lost all fear of death and lived more joyously than before. Needless to say, Swedenborg's claims met with considerable scepticism among his contemporaries. All the same, his influence was both deep and widespread. Poets such as William Blake found in Swedenborg confirmation that the world accessed by imagination is just as real as the material world perceived by the senses. Such men were, like the alchemists, working alone to find their way to sublime experiences. The days of communal experience (such as that of the Eleusis initiates and the Pythagoreans) had long gone, and in a world increasingly seen in terms of Newtonian physics and rationalism the experience of divinity flowed into the channel of individual experience and inner revelation.

THE ENGLISH PAGAN

This was the period known as the Age of Reason or of Enlightenment, when philosophical thought concentrated upon the virtues of rationality applied to questions such as the relationship between the individual and the state. Subjects such as the rights of man (and of women) became hot topics of debate. Philosophy – the love of wisdom – no longer pursued spiritual matters and would have been unrecognizable to Socrates and Plotinus. However, as if by a natural law, one man arose to bring back into the light of attention the wisdom of the ancient world. That man is Thomas Taylor (1758–1835), who became known as the English Pagan.

Taylor was a brilliant and hard-working scholar of the classics who took upon himself the life task of reviving the Neoplatonic wisdom and making it available in translation. Born into a poor family, he endured great hardship for years, working long hours and studying at night. Taylor's attempts to strike out by himself seemed doomed to failure. For example, he invented a 'perpetual flame' that he demonstrated at Freemason's Hall – unfortunately starting a small fire in the process. Eventually Taylor secured some rich patrons who funded his translations and enabled him to devote his energies entirely to translation. Like Ficino, he achieved feats of translation that would be far beyond the energy or capabilities of anyone not inspired by and in tune with the thought of the ancient world. Taylor gathered together the complete works of Plato and Aristotle and translated not only the major works of the Neoplatonists (Plotinus, Proclus, Iamblichus, Porphyry) but also the ancient Orphic Fragments and Hymns and the Chaldean Oracles. He wrote a lengthy treatise on the Orphic and Eleusinian Mysteries, explaining their symbolism in considerable detail.

The texts with which Taylor was working had, over time, come to contain inaccuracies and even gaps in places. Remarkably, his insight and understanding were such that he was able to correctly fill in many gaps, as later discoveries have confirmed. Taylor also used Ficino's Latin translations, recognizing Ficino as a fellow mystic and Neoplatonist. So thoroughly did Taylor live in the ancient world that he and his wife used to converse in ancient Greek and Taylor wrote hymns to the Greek gods in the Orphic style.

In a way, Taylor was lucky enough to ride the zeitgeist, for one aspect of the Age of Reason was that the ancient Greeks came to be seen as the inventors of logic and rational enquiry. The style of ancient Greece became all the rage in art and architecture, and Taylor was a part of this revival – although what he was writing was mystical rather than rational. Certainly he gained enough popularity to win the support of such luminaries as the Duke of Norfolk.

Taylor gave 12 lectures on the Platonic philosophy in the house of John Flaxman, one of Blake's patrons, and it is possible that Blake himself attended. Undoubtedly Taylor's thought influenced Blake, who illustrated one of Porphyry's works that he can only have known in Taylor's translation. Other poets too, including Shelley, Keats and (later) Yeats, were attracted to Taylor's understanding of the ancient wisdom. His influence extended as far as Madame Blavatsky's Theosophical Society, through the enthusiasm of her secretary G. R. S. Mead (who was himself to translate into English the *Corpus Hermeticum*).

All the same, such support and influence did not protect Taylor from ridicule during his life. He did not help his cause by being openly critical of the corrupt state of the Christian church, as he saw it, and unfortunately his translations are far from easy to read. Accurate they certainly are, but Taylor did not have the gift of simple and clear expression in English. What's more, he tended to lard his works with lengthy footnotes, frequently lashing out at his critics in no uncertain manner. But Taylor's belligerent tone sprang from his frustration that more people did not embrace the wisdom enshrined in the ancient writers: he must at times have felt very lonely.

If Thomas Taylor had not been born, what would have become of the ancient wisdom? Individuals such as Swedenborg and Blake would still have lived their mystical experiences, but knowledge of the true nature of Orphic wisdom in all its richness would have remained hidden. Taylor stands with Ficino as a figure of extraordinary importance; both men single-handedly preserved and revealed the Mysteries for their own and future generations. Such is the power of the hidden wisdom that it can safely entrust itself to such slender bridges between past and future.

FRIEND OF ANGELS

Six months before Thomas Taylor was born, England's greatest visionary poet and painter entered the world in London. William Blake (1757–

1827) suffered, like Taylor, from extreme poverty during his life and, also like Taylor, found patrons who helped him. Both men were critical of Christianity and hoped for a radical reform of society – after all, this was the period of the French and American Revolutions. But unlike Taylor, Blake saw visions from an early age. While Swedenborg visited heaven and hell, Blake found heaven in the humble streets of Lambeth and saw London transfigured into a divine city.

As a child of non-conformist parents, Blake was brought up on the Bible and educated at home. His first vision appeared at the early age of four, when the sight of God at the window sent him into a fit of screaming. At a later age he saw angels sitting in a tree on Peckham Rye,

The rebellious poet Percy Bysshe Shelley absorbed Platonic wisdom through the philosophical translations of Thomas Taylor and was inspired by William Blake's bold attitude.

but this vision brought him no good either, as his father threatened to beat him for telling lies. Undaunted, Blake developed an original visual imagination that was nourished by contact with non-material reality. In effect, all his pictures are visions.

Blake's parents recognized his artistic talent and when he was ten sent him to Henry Pars' drawing school, where he studied busts and drawings from antique subjects. This was the period of the Greek Revival. At the age of 14 Blake was apprenticed to Basire, the engraver to the Society of Antiquaries. Here again he was surrounded by the ancient world, which entered his imagination alongside biblical narratives. One further influence remained to make Blake's art what it was: Gothic architecture. When Blake was 16, Basire sent him to engrave the London churches, including Westminster Abbey. Here Blake experienced more visions and fell in love with the elegant and nature-inspired forms of Gothic.

In 1782 Blake embarked on married life with Catherine Boucher, who became his lifelong support and working partner. Catherine was illiterate, but Blake taught her to read and write; later she helped him produce his wonderful illustrated books of poetry and hand-tinted some of the illustrations. Poor Catherine did not have an easy life. During one period of particularly dire poverty, she found the only way she could impress upon the unworldly Blake the urgency of their crisis was to place an empty plate before him at dinner. For Blake resembled Thomas Taylor in his fiery, impulsive and fiercely independent temperament. Although he tried many times to make money by various artistic schemes, he never succeeded. Had it not been for his loyal patron, Thomas Butts, he and Catherine may well have starved, for what Blake was doing would never appeal to the masses.

AN ARTISTIC VISIONARY

Blake is unique in English art and literature for working in both poetry and art, and integrating the two. His poetry and pictures are direct expressions of his visionary insights: they are testaments to the secret wisdom, but couched in a style so very unusual that it is almost as difficult to understand as an alchemical text. Even his simplest verses conceal profound meanings. And Blake draws on many of the philosophers and writers whom we have studied, mingling all their influences into an extraordinary whole. The easiest way for a new reader to make sense of his work is to approach it through the lucid explanations offered by the Neoplatonic poet Kathleen Raine, who considered Blake her master. Raine's insights inform the following paragraphs.

Blake created a whole imaginative universe with a cast of divine characters and told its story through epic verse. His *Prophetic Books* draw on the Bible and Greek myth in order to create a new mythology through which he can rail against the crushing of the human spirit by reason and tyranny, then prophesy its final triumph. *Vala* or The Four Zoas retells the ancient story of Cupid and Psyche, first put in literary form by Apuleius in the second century CE. Apuleius was a Platonist and an initiate of several Mystery cults, including those of Dionysus and Isis, so the tale of Cupid and Psyche has a hidden meaning: it is the story of the soul's separation from divinity and the trials of its return. Blake retells this tale on a cosmic scale, setting it in a world where Urizen (reason – the demiurge or creator god) stands for the repression against which Luvah (Love or Cupid) must revolt.

We can see from this that Blake's mystical views were in harmony with those of the ancients. He called the secret wisdom 'The Everlasting

The 'dark Satanic mills' of industrialized society aroused Blake's anger: he hated to see humanity so enslaved in these foreboding commercial boxes.

Gospel', but it is a gospel that reinterprets Christianity in a radical way. Christ represents for Blake the divinity in all life: for 'everything that lives is Holy' (*Complete Writings*, p.199). Like the Pythagoreans, Blake considered the body to be like a tomb from which each person can only glimpse the true nature of the infinite world. 'For man has closed himself up, till he sees all things thro' narrow chinks of his cavern.' But if 'the doors of perception were cleansed, everything would appear to man as it is, infinite' (*Complete Writings*, p.154).

How do you know but ev'ry Bird that cuts the airy way,
Is an immense world of delight, clos'd by your senses five?
(*Complete Writings*, p.150)

And that is exactly how Blake himself saw the world, as 'all one continued Vision of Fancy or the Imagination' (Raine, p.102). For imagination, in Blake's view, was the faculty through which truth was revealed. 'The World of Imagination is the World of Eternity ... Infinite and Eternal, whereas the World of Generation ... is Finite and Temporal' (Raine, p.127).

No wonder Blake was so profoundly influential on later poets! Here he is, placing poets, artists and all those who live by the imagination in the position of being in touch with the truths of the spiritual world. He follows in the tradition of individualists such as Swedenborg who, in a society that fails utterly to acknowledge the hidden wisdom, must find their own way to it. Blake's bold attitude inspired the next generation of poets, the Romantics – Wordsworth, Shelley and Keats – who enjoyed living beyond the margins of polite society. And the great Irish poet William Butler Yeats revered Blake, as we shall see.

LIBERATION IN DELIGHT

Against the truths of imagination, Blake set the scientific laws of Newton that had created the Industrial Revolution and the famous 'dark Satanic Mills' (*Complete Writings*, p.481). City-dwellers suffered physical oppression in the hard work and deprivation of their lives, while the Church crushed their spiritual life under a burden of hypocrisy. Blake's vision of liberation is based on the holy nature of natural energy, which is *Eternal Delight* (*Complete Writings*, p.149). Wild animals such as tigers and lions symbolize in his writings this joyous force. But unfettered energy is not necessarily fierce: it only turns fierce when frustrated. In his book of children's verse, Songs of Innocence, Blake includes two poems, *The Little Girl Lost* and *The Little Girl Found*, that tell in simple form the myth of Persephone. In Blake's version, lions rescue the little girl, and when her parents eventually find her, they choose to remain in the wilderness with the animals. The two poems relate the Lesser and Greater Mysteries in Blake's own peculiar vision, and seem to be based partly on Thomas Taylor's essay on Eleusis.

Blake drew on Taylor's translations for several of his poems and paintings. His lyrical poem Thel, for example, is also based on the Persephone myth as well as on Plotinus' essay *On Beauty* and relates the fall of the soul from the divine world into the material world of birth and death. And in 1821, Blake made a beautiful and mysterious watercolour illustrating Porphyry's *Cave of the Nymphs*, the important text that describes souls entering the world through the Gate of Cancer and leaving to return to the Divine through the Gate of Capricorn. Such works are baffling without the Neoplatonic key to open them to the understanding, but to poets steeped in the Neoplatonic and magical tradition, such as Yeats, they were signs on the path to liberation.

Blake revered Milton, despite his Puritanism, and illustrated *L'Allegro* and *Il Penseroso* – which, as we have seen, are Milton's most Neoplatonic poems. There lies the clue to Blake's admiration, for he saw Milton as an initiate in spite of himself. Blake read *Paradise Lost* (which he also illustrated) as a tale of holy energy and desire being restrained and crushed by reason. But he noted, as have many others, that Milton wrote far more vividly about Satan and hell than about angels and paradise. So, claimed Blake, that was where Milton's sympathy really lay; 'he was a true Poet and of the Devil's party without knowing it' (*Complete Writings*, p.150).

Blake also illustrated Dante, and so enthusiastic was he to do so that he learned Italian in order to be able to read *The Divine Comedy*. But he disliked the cruelty of the punishments inflicted in Dante's version of hell: for Blake, hell is this world. And although Blake and Catherine belonged to the Swedenborgian Society, in the end Blake decided that Swedenborg too had been a victim of contemporary religion: 'a Samson shorn by the churches' (Raine, p.206). Only among the great Renaissance artists such as Botticelli and Michelangelo did Blake feel he was in the presence of untrammelled, divine energy. He based the elongated, curvilinear forms of his own art partly on these artists as well as on the shapes of Gothic sculpture. Also, he recognized them to be painting Mysteries. And that was also Blake's own life work, in his writing as well as his visual art.

Blake approached his death with as much cheerfulness as Swedenborg. He sat up in bed working right to the last, drawing a beautiful portrait sketch of Catherine just a few days before he died. At the last, 'His Countenance became fair. His eyes Brighten'd and he burst out Singing of the things he saw in Heaven' (Grigson, p.38). Catherine, when her own time came three years later, passed on with similar joy, calling out to Blake that she would soon be with him. For this couple the spiritual world was far more real than the delusive material world.

Blake epitomizes the life of a spiritual genius caught in a society that, with the development of mechanical science, had become inimical to the secret wisdom. His way out was through individual expression, which required a powerful personality and an acceptance of poverty. But not everyone is suited to tread such a lonely path. Later generations of seekers would find ways of banding together in imitation of the Eleusis initiates, creating secret societies devoted to occult understanding – and that is where we turn our attention next.

WILLIAM BLAKE WAS ahead of his time, proclaiming the divine nature of the imagination before those poets who came to be known as the Romantics adopted the same creed. Wordsworth, Shelley and Keats all sought to achieve transcendence through the intensity of their experiences. Wordsworth took a mystical view of nature, while Shelley read Thomas Taylor's translations of Plato and absorbed the ancient mystical view. Keats, a natural mystic, coined the memorable phrase 'Beauty is truth, truth beauty' in his lyric poem *Ode on a Grecian Urn*. It is significant that the Romantic view of a natural world infused with life and emotion came at a time when industrialization was creating polluted and teeming cities.

> O sages standing in God's holy fire
> As in the gold mosaic of a wall,
> Come from the holy fire, perne in a gyre,
> And be the singing masters of my soul.
> — W.B. Yeats, *Sailing to Byzantium*

HARD TIMES

The development of machinery capable of mass-producing goods such as textiles along with new transport systems able to move them around the country and abroad led to a vast social upheaval. Huge factories attracted the poor to work in towns that rapidly spread in an uncontrolled manner, with appalling living conditions for their inhabitants. Blake's 'dark Satanic mills' swallowed the lives of countless thousands of people, including children. Never before had human beings spent their days in such an artificial way, among steel machines, lit by gas, clothed in machine-woven cotton and – later – man-made textiles.

On top of this profound change came Darwin's work on evolution, proving that mankind had not been created according to the biblical account but that life had existed on earth for millions of years – and that mankind had evolved from apes. *On the Origin of Species* was published in 1859, setting out Darwin's theory of natural selection. Naturally, this shook the faith of many Christians. Although the Victorian era is seen as one of great piety, it seems that there was a perception that Christianity did not hold its own against the materialistic onslaught of industrialization and science. Hence there grew up a strong interest in alternative spiritualities, which tended, in this supremely materialistic period, to reflect their era.

In 1848, sisters Kate and Margaret Fox caused a sensation in America by claiming to have contacted the spirit of a man who had been murdered. In no time, spiritualism spread across the Continent and Britain. Seances became fashionable entertainment, mediums enjoyed fame (and notoriety), and the confusion between genuine and fraudulent practitioners provoked constant controversy. Along with spiritualism other, more familiar, occult studies thrived, such as astrology. Even alchemy found adherents once more.

In the face of the hard realities of the modern world, there grew up another culture in which occult studies were pursued by those who were grief-stricken or thrill-seeking, and town-dwellers looked for a new source of miracles in an age when materialism was already proving to be unsatisfactory and religion inadequate.

MYSTICISM FROM RUSSIA

Just three years after William Blake died with the vision of heaven before his eyes, a much more problematical mystic was born in Russia. Helena Blavatsky (1831–1891) was the daughter of a colonel and a successful novelist, and it could be said that she inherited from her parents a strong organizational ability and a vivid imagination. Accusations of fraud were thrown at her from early on in her career in spiritualism, yet despite Blavatsky's controversial claims her influence has endured to this day.

Helena Blavatsky shrouded her origins in mystery, but her ideas are still immensely influential.

We have seen how inspired individuals such as Swedenborg and Blake carried the ancient wisdom through the rationalistic and mechanical upheavals of the Age of Enlightenment. Their single voices were sufficient to ensure its survival, but different times need different methods. In effect, Europe was in a spiritual crisis. Single voices would no longer be heard above the roar of the machines: a larger movement was needed to preserve the hidden wisdom. Blavatsky was a leading figure in this 'spiritual counter-culture'. As Western society became more deeply entrenched in the results of the Industrial Revolution, Blavatsky revived the archaic idea of an initiatory society, a school of Mysteries.

Madame Blavatsky led a colourful life, the factual truth of which is hard to unravel. She married very early but ran away from her husband after only a few months. Once free from her husband and family she embarked on worldwide travels, including (according to her) a spell in Tibet, where she learned occult lore at the feet of mysterious lamas she called the Brothers. This was at a time when the number of Westerners who had penetrated Tibet could be numbered on one hand.

Having imbibed the wisdom of the East, Madame Blavatsky made her way to New York, where she began to gain fame as a medium in the spiritualist movement. Here she met a journalist, Henry Steel Olcott, who was interested in writing about spiritualism. Together with a group of like-minded people, Blavatsky and Olcott founded the Theosophical Society in 1875 as a new Mystery cult that sought to bring out the one basic truth behind all religions. Blavatsky – always a strong character – had found that the passive role of medium did not give full rein to her powers. She was far more suited to fill the role of teacher or guru and so she developed a system that demanded positive involvement, discipline and will.

THE THEOSOPHICAL MOVEMENT

Theosophy drew on both the Western Mystery tradition and the religions of the East to create a distinctive esoteric history of mankind. The syncretistic approach of the Theosophical Society can be seen in Olcott's own interests, for not only did he found Buddhist schools in India but he was also given honorary membership of the Brahmin caste in honour of his services to Hinduism – even though Buddhism does not recognize the hierarchy of the caste system. Olcott was president of the Theosophical Society until the time of his death.

Between them, Blavatsky and Olcott forged a system of thought that drew on many esoteric sources while retaining a distinctly nineteenth-century flavour. Blavatsky was well aware of the lure of the exotic: what with her own Russian origins and colourful life and talents (apparently including clairvoyance and telepathy) and her claims of deriving wisdom from the mystic East, she ensured that theosophy had plenty in it to intrigue. The society's name originates with Neoplatonism and means 'divine wisdom' or 'wisdom of the divine'. Indeed, some of the basic tenets of theosophy are drawn from Plato and the Neoplatonists, not least the idea that the soul is imprisoned in the body. Theosophy agrees with the ancient wisdom that the core of every human is a divine spark, and it also – like Plato – teaches reincarnation. Humans who have gained a

Henry Olcott helped found Theosophy and blended Indian religions with Western mysticism.

high degree of spiritual evolution act as guides to the rest of humanity. The Theosophical Society, however, laid more emphasis on the Eastern religions and philosophies, one of their main aims being a systematic study of these systems. They had two other purposes: to form a Brotherhood of Humanity and to investigate the psychic powers that were causing such a sensation in seance parlours at the time.

This is where the story begins to get murky. Blavatsky claimed that she had gained her esoteric wisdom from two highly evolved beings dedicated to the spiritual development of mankind, whom she called Mahatmas. Usefully for her, these Mahatmas resided out of most Western people's reach in India and Tibet. When Blavatsky was staying at her friend A. P. Sinnett's home in Simla, the Mahatmas wrote them letters conveying some of their exotic Eastern wisdom. They also confided to Blavatsky the spiritual history of the world, which she set down at length in two volumes called *The Secret Doctrine* (published in 1888).

In a way, we are now right back at Plato's Timaeus with its creation story, for the first volume of *The Secret Doctrine* describes the beginning and evolution of the universe. The second volume sets forth a description of humanity's evolution through vast periods of time. Various 'root races' are said to have lived in such mythical places as Atlantis, with 'sub-races' evolving to form a complicated pattern of influences. There is no doubt that Blavatsky's scheme has uncomfortable undertones of racism for a modern reader, but it was just the kind of dense and exotic scheme that leisured Victorians lapped up. And it came naturally to them to regard some races as inferior – after all, this was the age of colonialism.

But what does the history of the universe and mankind have to tell us about our own inner light and our return to the Divine? Although theosophy includes meditation, the emphasis is much more on study of Blavatsky's theories. The ancient simplicity of direct experience such as the Eleusinian initiates enjoyed has little part to play here: instead, there are Blavatsky's books as a kind of scripture to be read and believed. Even today, theosophists continue reinterpreting works such as *Isis Unveiled* and *The Secret Doctrine*.

The problem faced by anyone claiming unique revelation is that they are casting themselves in the role of a religious leader. The expectations of both followers and critics are thus very elevated indeed, and human flaws attract a huge amount of attention. The brightest light casts the darkest shadow. Even from her early days as a medium, Blavatsky had drawn accusations of fraudulency and her career was marked by controversy. One of her most charismatic disciples, Rudolf Steiner, ended by developing his own movement, anthroposophy. During her life, Blavatsky had the strength of character to hold the society together fairly coherently, but after her death in 1891 the history of the society is one of constant schism. Various theosophical societies thus came to exist in India, the United States, Germany and England, all with slightly varying interpretations of Blavatsky's doctrine.

THE LOSS OF KRISHNAMURTI

The most dramatic split was caused by C. W. Leadbeater, one of the prominent members of the Theosophical Society's main headquarters in Adhyar, India. In 1909, Leadbeater (who was notorious for enjoying the company of young boys) claimed a young and beautiful Indian boy, Jiddu Krishnamurti (1895–1986), as the incarnation of Maitreya, the new spiritual World Teacher. Krishnamurti was groomed for stardom. However, during a retreat in California he enjoyed time away from Leadbeater's influence. That period of independent contemplation, followed by the death of his beloved brother, produced a profound, though painful, spiritual awakening. In 1929 he publicly announced his separation from the theosophical movement. Krishnamurti spent the rest of his life as an independent spiritual teacher, effectively fulfilling the role that Leadbeater had claimed for him, but as an independent devotee of the divine wisdom.

The loss of Krishnamurti was a severe blow to the Theosophical Society. However, the lure of secret knowledge exerted a powerful enough force to ensure its survival and today there is a whole range of organizations claiming affiliation with or direct descent from the Society. Undoubtedly theosophy set the stage for the development of what is now known as the New Age movement, whose practitioners tend to bring together an eclectic mixture of esoteric influences rather than adhering to a single philosophical or religious system.

Perhaps the Krishnamurti story illustrates the unexpected ways in which the Society really worked for the good and for the passing on of secret wisdom. Other theosophists took various spiritual routes.

Chosen to be a spiritual World Teacher, Krishnamurti broke away from theosophy to find his own path.

For example, G. R. S. Mead (1863–1933) abandoned his teaching job to be Blavatsky's secretary until her death and to edit the Theosophical Society's magazine, *Lucifer*. Mead was a Cambridge-educated classicist who developed a profound interest in Gnosticism. He became the first modern scholar to make available translations of Gnostic texts, famously publishing a translation of the *Corpus Hermeticum* (1906) that remains unrivalled today. Mead devoted himself to studying the intermingling of philosophical and religious thought during the early centuries of Christianity, including of course the Neoplatonic strand. His work stands as proof that exemplary scholarship can be used to express a profound mystical insight. Although Mead is comparatively unsung today – for he was not a flamboyant character – his work provided an extremely important channel through which ancient texts of the hidden wisdom could flow.

MYSTICISM AND THE ARTISTS

Theosophy also infiltrated the arts, including poetry, as we shall see later with Yeats. The Russian composer Alexander Scriabin (1872–1915) studied theosophy as well as other spiritual ideas, including Neoplatonism. He expressed his mysticism through music, developing a 'mystic chord' and working with colour to create a unity of experience. Towards the end of his life he conceived the somewhat alarming project of a piece of music to be played in the Himalayas that would cause Armageddon and the consequent renewal of the world. Perhaps fortunately, he did not complete Mysterium before he died, although a performance version has since been patched together.

Although the French composer Eric Satie (1866–1925) did not embrace theosophy, he too was deeply influenced by the ancient wisdom – in his case, Rosicrucianism, Gnosticism and Renaissance magic. This delightfully eccentric man was another musical innovator who is now hailed as the inventor of ambient music. The titles of his atmospheric piano pieces give away his interests, including Gymnopédies, Gnossiennes and Vexations. The first refers to ancient Greek religious rituals and the second to Gnostic wisdom. Vexations is extraordinary – a short piano piece to be repeated no less than 840 times. Pianists who have attempted the piece report that it has an exhausting yet meditative effect and that they pass into a trance state. Satie derived the title from a book on alchemy by Paracelsus called *Coelum Philosophorum* or Book of Vexations. The vexations of which Paracelsus writes are the deadly repetitive processes the alchemist must follow, often without any obvious result and with no promise of success except for the inner refinement of spirit that such a discipline produces. Here Satie experiments with using music to create a mystical experience akin to that of practising alchemy. The piece is not really intended for listeners but for the benefit of the solo pianist.

Theosophy did, however, deeply influence other creative people at the turn of the century. One of them is Piet Mondrian (1872–1944). This Dutch artist famously developed a style of painting based on a grid made with primary colours and black on a white ground – a seemingly simple system that is in fact extremely difficult to imitate successfully. Mondrian was a highly spiritual person who became interested in theosophy around 1908. Henceforth it was to influence his art, and although Mondrian had not yet developed his mature style at this point he did begin to produce paintings that in form and content are extremely mystical. Even his abstract grids have hidden meanings, encoding the secret forces that determine the way nature reproduces itself and pointing up the eternal tension between physical and spiritual reality.

In fact, art and music at this time were awash with mystics. Gustav Holst studied astrology and wrote *The Planets* (1914–16), which is celebrated as the most frequently played piece of music by an English composer. Meanwhile Wassily Kandinsky, who paved the way for abstract art, published his theories on the spiritual impact of painting in *Concerning the Spiritual in Art* (1911). According to Kandinsky, the artist has a duty to inspire those who see his work to move from materialism towards spirituality; the colour and form of an artwork can move the soul. Kandinsky himself used meditative techniques while working. For example, while painting his monumental panel Composition VI, which he meant to evoke the whole process of birth, death and rebirth in the form of a vast flow of water, Kandinsky repeated the word 'flood' like a mantra. By this means he felt his way into the subject of the painting and finished it in a true deluge of inspiration within a mere three days.

These men were just a few of a number of creative people who, although not necessarily in touch with each other, were all infusing their work with ideas garnered from nineteenth-century spiritual movements. Even when they were unaware of what they were doing, their enduring works gave – and still give – glimpses into an experience so unfamiliar to many that they fail to recognize it as spiritual. However, the message is there for anyone who is willing to open his or her heart and soul.

So we see that theosophy and other mystical systems found their way into the arts in much the same way that Taylor's translations of the Neoplatonists affected Blake and the Romantic poets. It is almost as if Blavatsky had drawn on forces that were powerful enough to find their own way of expression quite apart from how she had originally intended. But there were other influences at work as well, and first among them was another secret society: one that concerned itself with ritual magic that drew on John Dee's conversations with angels. The twilight years of the nineteenth century gave birth to the Hermetic Order of the Golden Dawn.

RUBY ROSE AND CROSS OF GOLD

If Blavatsky's Theosophical Society forged the New Age movement, then the Hermetic Order of the Golden Dawn inspired a whole range of twentieth-century occult disciplines based on ritual magic, including Wicca and Aleister Crowley's Thelema. The history of the Order is at least as murky and complex as that of Blavatsky's Society.

The story goes that a Masonic scholar called Kenneth Mackenzie came into possession of a collection of manuscripts written in the code developed by the Renaissance occultist Trithemius. A fellow Mason, William Westcott, decoded them to discover that they formed a graded series of tuition in occult philosophy and practical magic very much according to Renaissance practice. There was also a name and address of a woman in Germany, one Anna Sprengel. In 1887 Westcott wrote to her and received in reply a charter to found the Golden Dawn, which he and his colleagues William Woodman and MacGregor Mathers promptly did. They organized the society along the lines suggested by the material in the manuscripts, which (unsurprisingly, given their origin) was a series of initiations in the manner of the Masons. The main difference was that the Golden Dawn accepted women as members on equal terms alongside men.

Notorious Aleister Crowley

There were allegedly three ascending Orders, the Golden Dawn being the Outer one. That was followed by a second, Inner order – and there was an invisible Third Order made up of mysterious Secret Chiefs who seemed to be identical with Blavatsky's Mahatmas. Anna Sprengel had received her instructions from these Chiefs, so when she dropped out of contact in 1891 the Golden Dawn initiates faced a problem. How were they to receive further instruction so that they could advance through the grades? Mathers solved this by claiming to have contacted the Secret Chiefs, who telepathically transmitted knowledge and instructions to him. He thus wrote the rituals for the second, Inner order, which was called Ruby Rose and Cross of Gold. The basic idea was the ancient Neoplatonic one of divine power pouring down through the universe through connecting series of channels: in the same way, occult knowledge was to be filtered down to the initiates from higher levels.

The Golden Dawn had a huge appeal to those who wished to be involved in ritual magic with life-changing potential, and in the first decade of its existence several temples were founded. However, just as with the Theosophical Society, schisms eventually ruptured the Dawn. Mathers championed Aleister Crowley despite vigorous opposition, and that led to splinter groups breaking away and forming similar groups under different names. Yet the Golden Dawn – or rival groups claiming to derive from it – still exists in various temples across the world. As in theosophy, its appeal is not only broad but also enduring.

What is the magic that the Golden Dawn works? It draws upon many of the sources we have considered earlier, a large part of it originating with John Dee's angel magic. It has strong links with the knowledge enshrined in Freemasonry as well as with the Rosicrucian groups that sprang up shortly before the founding of the Golden Dawn. Kabbalah is included in the course of study, as well as astrology and alchemy. All these subjects served to give the original initiates a sense of having power to manipulate nature personally, in direct contrast to the brutality of the industrial forces that defined their (and our) world. The Golden Dawn magicians were using magic that would be familiar to a Renaissance magus such as Ficino or Pico della Mirandola. However, whereas Ficino and Pico would have worked alone, the Golden Dawn drew up rituals that required a group of participants, thus creating the need for a supportive social structure.

What is more, they were acting in the context of a society that no longer supported a belief in occult reality.

ORPHEUS IN IRELAND

The Golden Dawn provided the setting for one last magus to revive the true aim of the ancient Mysteries and attempt to unite his soul with the Divine while still alive.

Nearly three millennia after Orpheus charmed humans and animals with his song, the Irish poet William Butler Yeats (1865–1939) attempted to do exactly the same thing. Yeats was the foremost Irish poet of his day. Through his poetry, his political activity, his revitalization of the Irish theatre and above all his devotion to Celtic mythology, he exercised such a powerful influence on Irish culture that it still reverberates today, a century and a half after his birth. Yet Yeats would now be remembered very differently were it not for a strange series of events springing from his lifelong involvement in ritual magic.

Yeats was born in Dublin and nurtured an interest in mysticism from an early age. By the time he was twenty he was presiding over the Dublin Hermetic Society, and within another five years he had dipped his toe into the Theosophical Society and taken the basic initiation of the Hermetic Order of the Golden Dawn in London. He was to remain a member of this Order for about thirty years, rising steadily through the ranks to positions of power and influence. When Mathers sent Aleister Crowley to take control of the London temple, Yeats was prominent in the faction that repulsed him. By 1900 Yeats was in charge of the Isis/Urania temple in London. He declared proudly to his many friends, 'The mystical life is the centre of all that I do and all that I think and all that I write.' (Kelly and Domville, vol.1, p.221)

Yeats took very seriously the oaths that Golden Dawn initiates were required to swear. One oath mingles magic with psychology: the initiate promises that he or she will 'prosecute the Great Work: which is to obtain control of the nature and power of my own being' (Raine, *Yeats the Initiate*, p.182). There is an echo here of the motto carved over Apollo's temple at Delphi: 'know thyself'. To do this, the initiate swears to make magical contact with his or her personal daimon, the guardian spirit of which Ficino wrote. Yeats will have vowed 'to purify and exalt my spiritual Nature that with the Divine Aid I may at length attain to be more than human, and thus gradually rise and unite myself to my higher and divine Genius' (Regardie et al, p.106). Another oath is cast in Christian terms: 'to establish closer and more personal relations with the Lord Jesus' (Raine, *Yeats the Initiate*, p.182). In other words, the initiate is both committing to a study of his or her own unconscious or occult powers, and setting out on the ancient mystic path to union with the Divine.

Much of Yeats' poetry cannot be understood without an acknowledgement that its symbolism and intention is directly magical. His early lyrical poems are saturated with symbols such as the Rosy Cross and an atmosphere of mysticism, here in *The Secret Rose*:

> Far-off, most secret, and inviolate Rose,
> Enfold me in my hour of hours; where those
> Who sought thee in the Holy Sepulchre,
> Or in the wine-vat, dwell beyond the stir
> And tumult of defeated dreams.

In an era when Blake's poetry was not widely appreciated, Yeats was devoted to it, considering himself Blake's spiritual disciple. He helped publish the first printed edition of Blake's *Prophetic Books* in 1893. And like Blake, Yeats studied Swedenborg's copious writings on the spiritual worlds, although (again following Blake) in later years his interest cooled off. Being Irish, Yeats also had a third source of ancient wisdom at his disposal: that of the rich and poetic Celtic mythology. No reader of his poetry can get far before encountering Druids, the hero Cuchulain and the mythical, godlike race of the Tuatha dé Danann.

YEATS IN LOVE

Yeats was a passionately romantic young man, and age did not moderate his outlook. Many of his poems celebrate his hopelessly unrequited love for Maud Gonne. Although Maud joined the Golden Dawn she did not stay long, preferring a more active life stirring up political dissent. She refused repeated proposals of marriage, driving Yeats to illness and despair. At the age of fifty Yeats turned his romantic attention to Iseult,

Maud's daughter from an early and unwise liaison. She also rejected him.

This final blow seems to have marked a mystical turning point that brought Yeats onto the right life path. He promptly – even rashly – courted and married Georgie Hyde Lees, a long-time acquaintance with an interest in psychic research. He was not simply acting on the rebound, for he had sound astrological reasons for getting married by October 1917. Yeats was a skilled astrologer and had long ago seen that the transits and progressions to his horoscope for this month were crucial. Nor was his choice of bride a casual one: he knew Georgie well enough to have acted as sponsor on her initiation into the Golden Dawn. Georgie, who had a profound interest in the occult, was far more committed to the secret society than Maud had been. By the time of their marriage, she and Yeats had reached the same grade ('6=5') of adeptship. In a very real way their marriage was a mystical one, both partners being well aware that their shared interest in magic would be a strong bond between them. They could hardly know, however, how profoundly alchemical this marriage would be: Yeats would be creatively revitalized and find a powerful and unique new voice in which to write some of the finest verse of the twentieth century.

But first there was a dark period to weather, just as in alchemy the nigredo precedes the later stages of creating the philosopher's stone. Yeats was still obsessed with Iseult, and once he had realized there was not even a faint possibility of marrying her, he immediately fell into a profound depression. With uncanny intuition, George (as Yeats always called her) attempted to dispel his gloom by trying some automatic writing. The first sentence she produced reassured Yeats that he had married the right woman, for it said: 'What you have done is right for both the cat and the hare.' George identified with cats to the point of dreaming repeatedly that she was one, and the wild hare is a suitable symbol for Iseult. It does not seem to have occurred to Yeats that George could have produced this sentence consciously or otherwise for her own reasons – or that the hare is associated with witchcraft and might be intended as a slight on Iseult Gonne.

So excited was Yeats by this experiment that he and George settled down to devote a few hours each day to her trance work. The 'communicators' were quite specific about their purpose; they announced, 'We have come to give you metaphors for poetry,' (Yeats, *A Vision*, p.8). Indeed, from this point onwards Yeats does seem to have developed a new sense of confidence and power in his poetry, forging an identity not only for himself but for his country too during a time of revolutionary upheaval. Rarely can such an important and influential body of work have arisen out of so esoteric an event. Yeats in effect announced his new esoteric purpose in the title of the first book of poetry he published following his marriage: *The Wild Swans at Coole* (1919). The communicators had chosen to give Yeats the image of the swan, allowing him to take on the mantle of Orpheus, who was reborn as a swan. Yeats later enriched the image by adopting it as the emblem of ancient Greek spiritual wisdom in contrast to the dove of Christianity.

THE WISDOM OF ANCIENT MASTERS

But what was Yeats trying to accomplish as a magician? On an exoteric level, his poetry deals with the Irish identity, the cataclysmic Easter Rising of 1916 and its aftermath, his own emotional life and the sad process of ageing. Yet within this outer shell lies a deeper level of meaning. For Yeats was following ancient masters: he mentions Empedocles, Pythagoras, Plato and Plotinus. In Golden Dawn parlance, he was attempting to become an Adept: one who achieves union with the Divine through a psychological experience of death during life. The twentieth-century poet was trying to follow Orpheus' trail down to the Underworld: we are back in the world of the Orphic and Eleusinian Mysteries.

Before meeting George, Yeats had read hardly any Greek philosophy. George, however, was extremely well-read in the ancient wisdom masters. Once Yeats started checking through her library to see if the mysterious communicators were perhaps no more than half-remembered fragments of Plato, he was hooked. Among much else, George possessed Thomas Taylor's translations of Plotinus. Yeats not only devoured Taylor but also went on to read the new and more accessible version of Plotinus by his fellow Irishman Stephen MacKenna. Then he went 'from Plotinus to his predecessors and successors whether upon her list or not' (Yeats, *A Vision*, p.20). For the next four years Yeats immersed himself in the most ancient and pure sources of the secret wisdom. In *A Vision* he mentions not only Plotinus but also Empedocles and Heraclitus, John Dee and the mystic poets Dante and Blake.

Thanks to George, Yeats became so completely involved in the secret wisdom that he began to see himself as a link in the Golden Chain of adepts. That meant focusing more on his inner world, and Yeats consciously modelled his life on the ideal Hermetic philosopher living in a lonely tower of whom Milton wrote in *Il Penseroso*. In 1915, Yeats bought a ruined Norman tower in Sligo, Thoor Ballylee. This tower became for Yeats both a retreat and a symbol of his lonely yet noble calling as a poet and mystic. In 1928 he published a book of poetry called *The Tower* that included several meditations on his home and its meanings, spelling out his vision of himself as a Platonic philosopher:

> A winding stair, a chamber arched with stone,
> A grey stone fireplace with an open hearth,
> A candle and a written page.
> Il Penseroso's Platonist toiled on
> In some like chamber, shadowing forth
> How the daemonic rage
> Imagined everything.
> (*Meditations in Time of Civil War*)

In these words Yeats abolishes time. He describes living as frugally as Milton's Platonist or indeed as Plotinus or Pythagoras: he is identifying as completely as possible with the ancient tradition. In that context it is important to note that a recurring theme of Yeats' poetry at this time is the pressing need to advance his spiritual growth now that he is growing old.

The strong sense of urgency he felt is evident in the following extract:

> Now shall I make my soul,
> Compelling it to study
> In a learned school
> Till the wreck of body...
> Seem but the clouds of the sky
> When the horizon fades.
> (*The Tower*)

Yeats' collection *The Tower* includes one of his most famous poems, *Sailing to Byzantium*. The key to this poem is the contrast between the endless round of birth and death that the poet describes in the first verse and his final vision of an eternal life in a state of aesthetic perfection. What he has in mind is Plato and his theory of a spiritual world full of perfect ideas, from which the imperfect and impermanent physical forms that we see are copied. Hence Yeats writes of 'flesh, fish or fowl' as 'those dying generations' and longs instead to free himself from the 'mortal dress' of his body and take the form of an exquisite golden bird, an image of perfection.

A POET'S VISION

Meanwhile, Yeats and George continued their automatic writing sessions and Yeats gradually built up from the communications a coherent body of esoteric knowledge. He published this under the title *A Vision* in 1925. This book is surely one of the strangest ever to have issued from a major poet's mind. Perhaps influenced by the orderly ritualized magic of the Golden Dawn, Yeats made of George's trance communications a theory of historical cycles and a system for describing all possible types of human psychology. Readers of Yeats' poetry who are baffled by his frequent mention of 'gyres' will find the meaning in *A Vision*. Yeats saw historical eras as rising and falling in a harmonious yet violent rhythm, one civilization rising as another falls. He symbolized this by the complex motions of two interpenetrating cones spinning in opposite directions: these are the gyres. In his apocalyptic poem *The Second Coming*, Yeats describes the twentieth century according to his theory:

> Turning and turning in the widening gyre
> The falcon cannot hear the falconer;
> Things fall apart; the centre cannot hold;
> Mere anarchy is loosed upon the world.

The birth of Christ 2,000 years ago called forth an opposing force whose time has now come:

> What rough beast, its hour come round at last,
> Slouches towards Bethlehem to be born?

Yeats' theory of human psychology uses a different cycle: that of the phases of the moon. He explains the cycle in poetic form in *The Phases of the Moon*, a poem written as a conversation between two Irish magi who pass by Thoor Ballylee and gently mock Yeats for sitting up at nights poring over his books in search of wisdom.

A Vision is a difficult read even for those familiar with esoteric concepts and writings. We can, however, note that Yeats' gyres hold reflections of Pythagorean mystical mathematics and the esoteric architectural details of the great cathedrals, such as the maze at Chartres. Yeats and George seem to have had a great deal of private fun out of their systems, and would be heard discussing merrily which phase of the moon described a new acquaintance.

Yeats felt that *A Vision* was at least as important as his celebrated collections of poetry. And yet, despite the fact that it is a considerable esoteric achievement, it ends on a rather poignant note. For Yeats was a true mystic who realized that, while systems and rituals have their place as means for focusing the mind, if over-indulged they can take the place of actual direct mystical experience of the Divine – and that experience was what Yeats longed for. He had nursed doubts about magical rites for many years. In a pamphlet written for Golden Dawn members in March 1901 he questions the value of ritual:

> Was Plotinus one of a 'group' organized on the 'globular sephiroth' when he was thrice united with God while still in the body? It is by sorrow and labour, by love of all living things, and by a heart that humbles itself before the Ancestral Light…that men come to Adeptship.

This is why the two characters in *The Phases of the Moon* laugh at Yeats: they know that arcane systems of learning will only take the adept part of the way. Yeats most deeply wished to have Plotinus' experience of making the journey beyond the planetary spheres, to reunite his soul with the Divine. Paradoxically, that means fully accepting one's own humanity, messy as it is. Yeats eventually realized what he must do, and expressed it thus in his poem *The Circus Animals' Desertion*:

> I must lie down where all the ladders start,
> In the foul rag-and-bone shop of the heart.

Sage in slippers. Whether or not Yeats achieved union with the Divine, he has much to teach us.

THE FINAL QUESTION

But what was the result of all Yeats' efforts? *A Vision* ends with a sense that he is still in the dark. Remarking that perhaps he is too old to receive enlightenment, he ends on a question – and this question is important, for it takes us right back to the beginning of our long tale. To understand it, you have to know that in *The Odyssey*, Homer describes Heracles (Hercules) as existing in the afterworld with the other dead souls only as an image. The true Heracles lives in heaven with the gods. Why is that? Because, famously, Heracles had been initiated at Eleusis and therefore did not suffer the fate of ordinary souls. In *A Vision*, Yeats asks:

> Shall we follow the image of Heracles that walks through the darkness bow in hand, or mount to that other Heracles, man, not image, he that has for his bride Hebe?

Here Yeats is affirming the unbroken chain that leads from the earliest participants in the Mysteries to himself, the chain that we have followed in this book. And yet, he hesitates between heaven and the Underworld. In the last letter that Yeats ever wrote, to his friend Lady Elizabeth Pelham, he sums up his mystical achievement:

> It seems to me that I have found what I wanted. When I try and put it all into a phrase I say, 'Man can embody truth but he cannot know it.'
>
> (Foster, vol. 2, p.650)

So it seems that the best that Yeats, the last magus, could do was to affirm his faith that the truth of life could be reached – but not known. He did not achieve the heights that the great mystics of the ancient world knew, and he may even have considered himself a failure. Yet, for us, he is invaluable. Yeats drew on the entire history of the secret wisdom and flooded his poetry with its images. In doing so he not only assured the survival of the Mysteries but also made much of that priceless wisdom available to his readers, whether or not they realize it. And he proves that great magi can still work in the world and communicate their knowledge through the traditional means – as long as we are prepared to make the considerable effort necessary to listen and understand. This is the true esotericism of the Mysteries: anybody can read Yeats but few can uncover the wisdom hidden in his poetry. The Mystery wisdom is as elusive and rare as it ever was – and as infinitely precious.

DISCIPLES OF THE LAST MAGUS

Although everybody who searches for a teacher or guru wants the highest and best, the esoteric rule is that the pupil needs a teacher whose wisdom is within his or her grasp. The teacher should, therefore, be only a few rungs further up the ladder than the pupil. Yeats may not be among the starry company who achieved unity with the Divine while in the body, but that makes him the ideal teacher for us. His teaching is difficult, but poetry works on a level of the personality that lies deeper than the intellect and simply reading Yeats can refine a sensitive reader's consciousness.

However, if poetry does not appeal there are many other routes to the secret wisdom through the proliferation of New Age movements. Many of these dilute the knowledge for the sake of reaching as broad an audience as possible, but it is there all the same. And the practice of alchemy continues to flourish both in Europe and the United States.

We have been on a long journey into the history of the secret wisdom, all the way across Europe and Asia, through cultures and historical periods so different they would barely recognize one other. Sometimes the wisdom has hung on the single thread of one person's experience, but it has always survived. This knowledge will never appeal to the majority, but there has always been a small core of seekers for whom the apparent reality of the world is not enough. You, since you have read this book, are one of them. Who knows: you may be the very person through whom the secret wisdom survives once more to entrance future mystics and keep alive the inner truth of our existence – that we are souls in exile in this material world, and that the way home is open to us.

SELECT BIBLIOGRAPHY

Chapter One: The Mysteries

Casavis, J. N. *The Greek Origin of Freemasonry*. (New York: Square Press, 1955).

Cory, I. P. *Ancient Fragments*. (London: William Pickering, 1832).

Grant, F. C. *Hellenistic Religions*. (Indianapolis: Bobbs Merrill, 1953).

Guthrie, W. K. C. *Orpheus and Greek Religion*. (London: Methuen, 1952).

Kerenyi, Karl. *Eleusis*. (Princeton NJ: Princeton University Press, 1967).

McGahey, Robert. *The Orphic Moment*. (Albany NY: State University of New York Press, 1994).

Mylonas, George. *Eleusis and the Eleusinian Mysteries*. (Princeton NJ: Princeton University Press, 1961).

Segal, Charles. *Orpheus*. (Baltimore: Johns Hopkins University Press, 1989).

Taylor, Thomas. *The Mystical Hymns of Orpheus*. (London: B. Dobell, 1896).

Wright, Dudley. *The Eleusinian Mysteries and Rites*. (Berwick, Maine: Ibis Press, 2003).

Chapter Two: The Philosophers

Barnes, Jonathan, trans. and ed. *Early Greek Philosophy*. (London: Penguin, 1987).

Kingsley, Peter. *Ancient Philosophy, History and Magic*. (Oxford: Clarendon Press, 1995).

Plato, trans. and ed. Tredennik, Hugh and Tarrant, Harold. *The Last Days of Socrates*. (London: Penguin, 1993).

Plato, trans. Hamilton, Walter. *Phaedrus*. (London: Penguin, 1973).

Plato, trans. Lee, H. D. P. *The Republic*. (London: Penguin, 2007).

Plato, trans. Hamilton, Walter. *The Symposium*. (London: Penguin, 1981).

Chapter Three: Christian Rapture

St Augustine, trans. Pine-Coffin, R. S. *Confessions*. (London: Penguin, 1973).

Euripides, trans. Vellacot, Philip. *The Bacchae and Other Plays*. (London: Penguin, 1973).

Freke, Timothy and Gandy, Peter. *The Jesus Mysteries*. (London: Thorsons, 1999).

Iamblichus, trans. Johnson, Thomas M. *The Exhortation to Philosophy*. (Grand Rapids, MI: Phanes Press, 1988).

Marinus of Samaria, trans. Guthrie, Kenneth S. *The Life of Proclus*. Grand (Rapids, MI: Phanes Press, 1986).

Plotinus, trans. MacKenna, Stephen, abridged Dillon, John. *The Enneads*. (London: Penguin, 1991).

Synesius of Cyrene, paraphrased Ionides, Alex C. *On Dreams*. (London and Aylesbury, 1929).

Chapter Four: Persian Magic

Afnan, Soheil M. *Avicenna: His Life and Works*. (London: Allen & Unwin, 1958).

Atiyeh, George. *Al-Kindi: The Philosopher of the Arabs*. (Rawalpindi: Islamic Research Institute, 1966).

Atkinson, David William. *The English Ars Moriendi*. (New York: Peter Lang, 1992).

Corbin, Henry, trans. Trask, Willard. *Avicenna and the Visionary Recital*. (Princeton NJ: Princeton University Press, 1990).

Dante, trans. Sisson, C. H. *The Divine Comedy*. (Oxford: Oxford University Press, 1998).

Fulcanelli, trans. Sworder, Mary. *Le Mystère des Cathédrales*. (London: Neville Spearman, 1971).

Gardner, Edmund Garratt. *Dante and the Mystics*. (London: Dent, 1913).

Scott, Walter (trans.). *Hermetica: The Writings Attributed to Hermes Trismegistus*. (Solos Press, 1993).

Kingsley, Peter. *In The Dark Places of Wisdom*. (Inverness, CA: Golden Sufi Press, 1999).

Majercik, Ruth. *The Chaldean Oracles*. (Leiden: Brill, 1989).

Marsilio Ficino, trans Sears, Jayne. *Commentary on Plato's Symposium on Love*. (Woodstock, CT: Spring Publications, 1985).

Sela, Schlomo. *Abraham ibn Ezra: The Book of Reasons*. (Leiden: Brill, 2007).

Tugwell, Simon (ed.). *Albert and Thomas: Selected Writings*. (New York: Paulist Press, 1988).

Chapter Five: Renaissance Magus

Marsilio Ficino, trans. Sears, Jayne. *Commentary on Plato's Symposium on Love*. (Woodstock, CT: Spring Publications, 1985).

Marsilio Ficino, trans. and ed. Caske, Carol V. and Clark, John R. *Three Books on Life*. (Binghampton, NY: Medieval & Renaissance Texts & Studies, 1989).

Marsilio Ficino, trans. and ed. Members of the Language Department of the School of Economic Science, London. *The Letters of Marsilio Ficino*. 7 vols. to date. (London: Shepheard-Walwyn Ltd, 1975–).

Plato, trans. Lee, H. D. P. *Timaeus*. (London: Penguin, 1965).

Shepherd, Michael, ed. *Friend to Mankind: Marsilio Ficino (1433–1499)*. (London: Shepheard-Walwyn, 1999).

Chapter Six: Secret Arts

Cassirer, Ernst, Kristeller, Paul Oskar, Randall, John Herman Jr., eds. *The Renaissance Philosophy of Man*. (Chicago: University of Chicago Press, 1948).

Garin, Eugenio, trans. Jackson, Carolyn and Allen, June. *Astrology in the Renaissance: the Zodiac of Life*. (London: Routledge and Kegan Paul, 1983).

Farmer, S. A. *Sycretism in the West: Pico's 900 Theses (1486)* (Tempe, AZ: Medieval & Renaissance Texts & Studies, 1998).

Gombrich, E. H. *Symbolic Images*. (London: Phaidon, 1993).

Hartt, Frederick. *History of Italian Renaissance Art* (London: Thames & Hudson, 1987).

Klibansky, Raymond, Panofsky, Erwin and Saxl, Fritz. *Saturn and Melancholy*. (London: Nelson, 1964).

Lehrich, Christopher. *The Language of Demons and Angels*. (Leiden & Boston: Brill, 2003).

Marsilio Ficino, trans. and ed. Members of the Language Department of the School of Economic Science, London. *The Letters of Marsilio Ficino*. 7 vols. to date. (London: Shepheard-Walwyn Ltd, 1975–).

Marsilio Ficino, trans. Sears, Jayne. *Commentary on Plato's Symposium on Love*. (Woodstock, CT: Spring Publications, 1985).

Seznec, Jean. *The Survival of the Pagan Gods*. (Princeton, NJ: Princeton University Press, 1972).

Trachtenberg, Marvin and Hyman, Isabelle. *Architecture: from Prehistory to Post-Modernism*. (London: Academy Editions, 1986).

Walker, D. P. *Spiritual and Demonic Magic from Ficino to Campanella*. (Notre Dame and London: University of Notre Dame Press, 1975).

Wind, Edgar. *Pagan Mysteries in the Renaissance*. (Oxford: Oxford University Press, 1980).

Chapter Seven: Speaking with Angels

Campanella, Tommaso, trans. and ed. Donno, Daniel J. *The City of the Sun*. (Berkeley, LA: University of California Press, 1981).

Dee, John, ed. Suster, Gerald. *John Dee: Essential Readings*. (Wellingborough: Crucible, 1986).

French, Peter. *John Dee: The World of an Elizabethan Magus*. (London: Routledge & Kegan Paul, 1972).

Greene, Thomas. 'Magic and Festivity', *Renaissance Quarterly*, 40, iv (1987).

Livergood, Norman D. *The Perennial Tradition*. (Dandelion Books, 2003).

Still, Colin. *The Timeless Theme*. (London: Ivor Nicholson and Watson, 1936).

Walker, D. P. *Spiritual and Demonic Magic from Ficino to Campanella*. (Notre Dame and London: University of Notre Dame Press, 1975).

Yates, Frances A. *Theatre of the World*. (London: Ark, 1987).

Chapter Eight: The Gold Makers

Churton, Tobias. *Magus: The Invisible Life Elias Ashmole*. (Lichfield: Signal, 2004).

Dee, John, ed. Suster, Gerald. *John Dee: Essential Readings*. (Wellingborough: Crucible, 1986).

Dee, John, trans. Shumaker, Wayne. *An Aphoristic Introduction*. (Berkeley: University of California Press, 1978).

Gilchrist, Cherry. *The Elements of Alchemy*. (Shaftesbury: Element Books, 1991).

Greene, Thomas. 'Magic and Festivity,' *Renaissance Quarterly*, 40, iv (1987).

Hamill, John. *The Craft: A History of Freemasonry*. (Wellingborough: Crucible, 1986).

Josten, C. H. *Elias Ashmole*. 5 vols. (Oxford: Clarendon Press, 1966).

Klossowski de Rola, Stanislas. *Alchemy, The Secret Art*. (London: Thames & Hudson, 1973).

Koestler, Arthur. *The Sleepwalkers*. (London: Hutchinson, 1979).

Roob, Alexander. *The Hermetic Museum: Alchemy and Mysticism*. (Cologne: Taschen, 1997).

Walker, D. P. *Spiritual and Demonic Magic from Ficino to Campanella*. (Stroud: Sutton Publications, 2000).

Yates, Frances A. *The Rosicrucian Enlightenment*. (London: Ark, 1986).

— Theatre of the World (London: Ark, 1987).

Chapter Nine: Sublime Rhyme

Blake, William, ed. Keynes, Geoffrey. *Complete Writings*. (Oxford: Oxford University Press, 1971).

Bullett, Gerald, ed. *Silver Poets of the 16th Century*. (London: Everyman, 1970).

Donne, John, ed. Smith, A. J. *The Complete English Poems*. (London: Penguin, 1973).

Dusen, Wilson van. *The Presence of Other Worlds*. (London: Wildwood House, 1975).

Gardner, Helen, ed. *The Metaphysical Poets*. (London: Penguin, 1966).

Grigson, Geoffrey. *Samuel Palmer*. (London: Kegan Paul, 1947).

Milton, John, ed. Wright, B.A. *Poems*. (London: Everyman, 1973).

Raine, Kathleen. *William Blake*. (London: Thames & Hudson, 1970).

Synnestvedt, Sig. *The Essential Swedenborg*. (New York: Twayne, 1970).

Chapter Ten: Twilight and Dawn

Blavatsky, Helena Petrovna. *Esoteric Writings of Helena Petrovska Blavatsky*. (London: Theosophical Publishing House, 1980).

Foster, R.F. *WB Yeats: A Life*. 2 vols. (Oxford: OUP, 1997–2003).

Graf, S. J. *WB Yeats: Twentieth Century Magus*. (York Beach, Maine: Samuel Weiser, 2000).

Morgan, Mogg. *Tankhem: Meditations on Tantrik and Egyptian Magick and the Mysteries of Seth, the Great Dragon*. (Oxford: Mandrake, 2003).

Raine, Kathleen. *Yeats the Initiate*. (London: Allen & Unwin, 1986).

Regardie, Israel, Monnastre, Cris, and Weschchke, Carl. *The Golden Dawn: A Complete Course in Practical Ceremonial Magic*. (St Paul, Minn: Llewellyn, 1985).

Yeats, W. B. *A Vision*. (New York: Collier Books, 1965).

Yeats, W. B. *'Is the Order R.R. & A.C. to Remain a Magical Order?'* Pamphlet for Golden Dawn, March 1901.

Yeats, W. B., ed. Jeffares, A. Norman. *Selected Poetry*. (London: Macmillan, 1975).

Yeats, W. B., ed. Kelly, John and Domville, Eric. *Collected Letters*. 4 vols. (Oxford: OUP, 1986–2005).

INDEX